Elaine Sigg

D0116793

Elaine Sigg

THIRD EDITION

The Collectors Encyclopedia of

DEPRESSION GLASS

BY

Gene Florence

Copyright: Gene Florence, Bill Schroeder, 1977

ISBN 0-89145-026-2

This book or any part thereof may not be reproduced
without the written consent of the author and publisher.

Published by

Collectors Books

Box 3009   Paducah, Kentucky 42001

Index

FOREWORD

Depression Glass as defined in this book is the colored glassware made primarily during the Depression years in the colors of amber, green, pink, blue, red, yellow, white and crystal. There are other colors and some glass included which was made before, as well as after this time; but primarily, the glass within this book was made from late 1920's through the 1930's. More attention is being given to some of the hand made glass of late, but mostly this book is concerned with the inexpensively made glassware turned out in quantity and given away as promotions or inducements to buy other products during that era known as The Depression.

Since the issuance of the second edition which has gone past the 50,000 mark in circulation, there have been changes in the collecting of Depression Glass. More and more attention is now being given the cheaper priced patterns and collectors are becoming aware of the better glassware made during this same period of time. There are a few such patterns included in this book.

Information gathered for the book has come from research, experience, fellow dealers, and over 100,000 miles of travel in connection with glassware as well as from readers who were kind enough and interested enough to share their knowledge with me. This last I particularly appreciate although the four postmen who have covered my route this past year obviously have not. For some reason they keep getting transferred.

Descriptions of the cover pieces are on the last page of this book.

PRICING

ALL PRICES IN THIS BOOK ARE RETAIL PRICES FOR MINT CONDITION GLASSWARE. THIS BOOK IS INTENDED TO BE ONLY A GUIDE TO PRICES AS THERE ARE SOME REGIONAL PRICE DIFFERENCES WHICH CANNOT REASONABLY BE DEALT WITH HEREIN.

You may expect dealers to pay from twenty to forty percent less than the prices quoted. Glass that is in less than mint condition, i.e. chipped, cracked, scratched or poorly molded, will bring very small prices unless extremely rare; and then, will bring only a small percentage of the price of glass that is in mint condition.

Prices have become pretty well nationally standardized due to national advertising carried on by dealers and due to the Depression Glass Shows which are held from coast to coast. However, there are still some regional differences in prices due partly to glass being more readily available in some areas than in others. Too, companies distributed certain pieces in some areas that it did not in others. Generally speaking, however, prices are about the same among dealers from coast to coast.

Prices tend to increase dramatically on rarer items and, in general, they have increased as a whole due to more and more collectors entering the field and people becoming more aware of the worth of Depression Glass.

One of the more important aspects of this book is the attempt made to illustrate as well as realistically price those items which are in demand. The desire was to give you the most accurate guide to collectible patterns of Depression Glass available.

MEASUREMENTS

All measurements in this book are exact as to manufacturer's listing or actual measurement where old catalogues do not give this information. You may expect variances up to ¼" on small items or ½" on larger items. There may be 1 to 5 ounce variations on tumblers and pitchers respectively due to mold variation or actual mold changes made by manufacturers.

Gene Florence, Jr.

ABOUT THE AUTHOR

Gene Florence, Jr., was born in Lexington, Kentucky, in 1944 and received his A.B. from the University of Kentucky in 1967, having majored in Mathematics and English. After teaching nine years in the Kentucky school system, he is presently leaving that to pursue his interest in glass to a greater extent.

This past summer he has been actively engaged in helping his mother convert her children's day nursery into Grannie Bear Antique Shop, the name being a hold over of the endearing term the 30 or so toddlers gave her. Naturally, should you be in Lexington, he'd appreciate your visiting her shop at 120 Clay Avenue. As he's often there, you might meet him.

Mr. Florence has been interested in "collecting" since childhood, beginning with the usual baseball cards and comic books and advancing to coin collecting, bottles and finally glassware.

He has written two other books on glassware, the Collector's Encyclopedia of Akro Agate and the Collector's Encyclopedia of Occupied Japan both of which have received warm praises from collectors in these fields.

Should you know of any unlisted pieces of glassware in the patterns shown in this book or have any information or questions you feel worthy of note, please feel free to write him at his new address: Gene Florence, 433 Hollywood Drive, Lexington, Kentucky 40502. Please enclose a self addressed stamped envelope if you wish a reply which should be immediately forthcoming now that there aren't the masses of school papers to grade.

ACKNOWLEDGEMENTS

Many have shared in the making of this all color third edition — all color save for some of the pattern shots which proved better in black and white for pattern identification purposes — something established only after painstakingly shooting them all in color, however. Some of those "many" are as follows: Cathy, my wife, again typist and editor; my family and in-laws, in general, for filling in the gaps during my absences at glass shows throughout the country; my sister, Lois, proofreader; John and Trannie Davis and sons, Mike and Bill, who shared their glass skills and home with us as a photographer's headquarters for photographing this third edition; Jerry and Connie Monarch who slaved at unwrapping and setting up glassware in 90 degree Georgia heat (or floodlight heat) for three hectic days so you could view all this; my publisher, Bill Schroeder; the photographer, Dana Curtis; Clyde Brugh and Doug Lucas who helped immeasurably in research and tracing down leads on glassware discoveries; and the wonderfully generous people who lent their treasures to be photographed. Among these were: John and Trannie Davis, Jerry and Connie Monarch, Joe, Jane, Joey and Judi Daniano, Joyce Denny, Geraldine Locaby, Mary Ensley, Inez Lawson, Mary Perrin, Jim and Sally DeBardelaben, Ernie Faver, Austin and Shirley Hartsock, Dot Morgan, Mrs. Kirby Dean, Leroy and Ruth Briley, Iris Slayton, Ellis Powell, Bud and Kathy Stultz, Mr. and Mrs. Edward Shaw, Helen Marshall, Irene Gilcrest, Arlene Showalter, Winona Fletcher, Vida Harris, Bill, Fern and Bradley Smith, Jean Scull, Al Broemel, Maxine and Ray Crawford, Mrs. Ethel Rhoads, and my parents, Mr. and Mrs. Gene Florence, Sr.

There is always the possibility of leaving someone out in a listing of that sort. If I have, it wasn't intentional nor am I unappreciative of your help. It's just as we go to the wire on this edition, I've overlooked your gesture of kindness. Forgive me if I have and be happy in the fact that thousands are benefitting from your effort in this behalf.

Additional copies of this book may be ordered from:
COLLECTOR BOOKS
Box 3009, Paducah, Kentucky 42001
or
The Author, Gene Florence
P.O. Box 7186H
Lexington, Kentucky 40502

at $14.95 Post Paid

Dealers and Clubs write for quantity discounts

ADAM

(pink, green, crystal, yellow) **JEANETTE GLASS COMPANY 1932-1934**

Thus begins our third journey with "Adam" into this garden of glassware known as Depression Glass. There are several new discoveries in this pattern since the last book; yet no new pieces of the spectacular and round shaped yellow can be reported. There are still only four plates, four saucers and seven cups known to exist. Perhaps tomorrow you will find some!

For the collectors of pink Adam, you have two new pieces to keep a weather eye out for in your travels. A round saucer and luncheon plate have turned up in separate places. Granted, I doubt they are plentiful; but my source for the luncheon plate said that its prior owner had had four others. The saucer could be a loner since its previous owner threw all the damaged ones like it away! (Have you given any thought to becoming a trash collector, pardon, sanitation engineer, lately?) My bet is that the round pieces of yellow and pink Adam were a trial run at the factory but that the squared motif lent itself more readily to the squared shape that was adopted. Hopefully, more of these oddities will show up.

Very few pieces of Adam are being found in crystal, but prices for crystal still remain much lower than those for pink due to a lack of demand for it.

The biggest jumps in prices have been made in pink Adam with the candy dish, vase and 5½ inch iced tea glass leading the parade. A number of green butter dishes have surfaced, or at least "a number" when you consider what was known before this. For comparison purposes, there were six green Adam butter dishes among the sixteen dealers at a show I attended in Tennessee yet only one pink.

The pink butter dish pictured is the Adam-Sierra combination. More of these have appeared since the one pictured on the cover of the last book; but they are still quite rare and represent quite a find for the butter dish collector. As such, they, naturally, still fetch a goodly sum. So far, none have been found in green.

That round based Adam pitcher in pink has been seen more this year and thus, the price has lowered somewhat. These round based pitchers are usually a paler pink color than the normal pink and they have occasionally been found in the company of a plain tumbler having the panels and curves of the regular Adam tumblers and pitchers, yet not having either the motif in the bottom or the flowers around the top. However, Adam collectors are reluctant to accept these tumblers as "true" Adam. Happiness would be finding one with either the motif or the flowers.

Few Adam lamps are seen though they certainly add interest to a collection. The base for the lamp was made from the sherbet which was frosted and notched at the top to accommodate the switch. If you're going to find one, try doing it with the original chimney-like bulb and metal cover intact as the latter are the Achilles heel. (See the lamp pictured in Floral for an idea of how the Adam lamp should look. The same company made both).

For those of you who are just beginning to collect, you might note that the lids to the sugar bowl and the candy dish in Adam are interchangeable.

	PINK	GREEN		PINK	GREEN
Ash Tray, 4½"	5.50	5.00	Pitcher, 8", 32 oz.	15.50	17.00
Bowl, 4¾" Dessert	4.25	4.00	Pitcher, 32 oz., Round Base	25.00	
Bowl, 5¾" Cereal	6.50	6.00	Plate, 6" Sherbet	2.00	2.00
Bowl, 7¾"	5.50	5.50	**Plate, 7¾" Sq. Salad	3.50	3.00
Bowl, 9" Covered	14.50	15.75	Plate, 9" Sq. Dinner	4.75	5.00
Bowl, 10" Oval	9.00	8.50	Plate, 9" Grill	3.75	3.75
Butter Dish & Cover	47.50	185.00	Platter, 11¾"	6.00	7.00
Butter Dish Combination			Relish Dish, 8" Divided	4.00	4.00
with Sierra Pattern	335.00		Salt & Pepper, 4" Footed	25.00	52.50
Cake Plate, 10" Footed	5.75	6.75	***Saucer, Sq. 6"	2.00	2.00
Candlesticks, 4" Pair	27.50	42.50	Sherbet, 3"	7.00	6.75
Candy Jar & Cover 2½"	23.50	47.50	Sugar	6.50	6.50
Coaster 3¾"	6.25	6.75	Sugar/Candy Cover	7.50	16.00
Creamer	6.50	6.50	Tumbler, 4½"	7.50	7.50
*Cup	6.50	6.00	Tumbler, 5½" Iced Tea	15.00	12.00
Lamp	60.00	60.00	Vase, 7½"	37.50	17.50

*Yellow   75.00
**Round Pink   25.00   Yellow   75.00
***Round Pink   20.00   Yellow   60.00

Please refer to Foreword for pricing information

AKRO AGATE CO.

1913-1951

The story of Akro Agate was too big for the one page in the second edition to really do more than scratch the surface. Children's dishes constitute only a very small portion of the total picture. Thus it was, after some further research, I decided to write a book on that topic alone, something that wasn't too hard since there is such a wealth of material to be covered. Devotees of this glassware have been warm in their praises for my efforts I'm happy to report.

Akro Agate has a fascinating history which has its start before the first World War and continues throughout the war years. This all encompassing glassware is fast becoming a worthy collectible, a fact which is being mirrored in the prices, naturally. As with Collectors Encyclopedia of Depression Glass, should the book just save you from selling a piece too cheaply that you presently own or if it clues you to the real value of a piece you find at a sale, the knowledge gained will have certainly "paid for" the book.

If you are interested in collecting glassware, I feel sure you will enjoy and gain from this book on Akro Agate. Write me about your "finds" as I am equally interested in the oddities being discovered in this.

Copies of this book may be ordered from

COLLECTOR BOOKS

Box 3009, Paducah, Kentucky 42001

or

The Author, Gene Florence

P.O. Box 7186H

Lexington, Kentucky 40502

at $8.95 post paid

Dealers and Clubs write for quantity discounts

AMERICAN PIONEER

(pink, green, amber, crystal)

LIBERTY WORKS
1931-1934

The tall lamp and covered jug in American Pioneer should have caught your eye on the front cover; if you did not recognize them then, now is a good time to start for this is a fast growing collectible pattern. The covered jug shown there was the "notorious" one pictured in the August 4, 1975 issue of Newsweek magazine; thus you're seeing a celebrity of sorts.

There are two styles of lamps, as you can see. One is 8½ inches tall and the other is a 5½ inch ball shaped lamp. Both were originally oil lamps; but you will find many that have been converted to electric use.

There are also two size covered jugs, 5 inch and 7 inch; and there are two sizes of candy jars, the 1½ pound and the 1 pound size. You may see the lid to the pound & half candy on the lower right of the photograph next to the pink cup and saucer. These lids are fairly tough to find and, in fact, they took what I thought was an unreasonably long time to round up for the picture. Notice the tall, handled candlesticks perhaps made for those who didn't trust either coal oil or electric lamps? The handles make them rather unusual at any rate.

That two handled platter comes with or without the indent. The indent is there to hold the shallow comport to constitute a cheese and cracker set or a handy server for dips in this day and age.

There are two sizes of creamer and sugars, 2¾ inch and 3½ inch high.

Those looking for a big covered dish should notice the one shown here and on the rare page at the back of the book.

The colors of pink and green vary in this pattern and will not match up nearly as well as will those in the Victory pattern, another of the new patterns in this edition.

A dresser set consisting of two cologne bottles and a powder jar and cover all resting on a round tray has been reported as well as a low and tall sherbet. These have eluded me; perhaps you'll have better luck.

There is only one style 7 inch vase shown; however, there are two others. One is straight up and down and the other has a crimped or fluted edge rather than the rolled edge of the one pictured.

I found a 4¼ tall, footed vase which holds 16 ounces and which I'll call a rose bowl for now.

AMBER, PINK, GREEN, CRYSTAL

Bowl, 5" handled	4.00
Bowl, 8¾" covered	30.00
Bowl, 9" handled	6.50
Bowl, console 10⅜"	20.00
Candlesticks, 6½" pair	27.50
Candy Jar and Cover, 1 lb.	25.00
Candy Jar and Cover, 1½ lb.	35.00
Cheese and Cracker Set (indented platter and comport)	13.50
Coaster, 3½"	4.00
Creamer, 2¾"	2.25
Creamer, 3½"	3.00
Cup	1.75
Dresser Set (2 cologne, powder jar, on indented 7½" tray)	40.00
Goblet, Wine, 4", 3 oz.	10.00
Goblet, Water, 6", 8 oz.	12.00
Ice Bucket, 6"	15.00
Lamp, 5½" round, ball shape	45.00
Lamp, 8½" tall	47.50
Pitcher, 5" covered urn	50.00
Pitcher, 7" covered urn	60.00
Plate, 8"	2.00
Plate, 11½" handled	5.00
Saucer	1.00
Sugar, 2¾"	2.25
Sugar, 3½"	3.00
Tumbler, 4", 8 oz.	8.00
Tumbler, 5", 12 oz.	10.00
Vase, rose bowl, 16 oz. 4¼", ftd.	30.00
Vase, 7", three styles, rolled, or crimped edge, straight	35.00

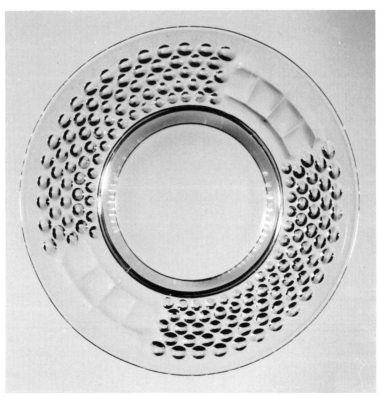

AMERICAN SWEETHEART

(pink, monax, cremax, red and blue) **MACBETH EVANS GLASS COMPANY 1930-1936**

How clever that "American" Sweetheart comes in red, white and blue! A lady told me her mom used to set the table every July 4 with said three colors. Wow!

From my observation, I believe the blue 8 inch American Sweetheart plates to be far rarer than the red. Blue prices have increased but not as dramatically as in the past. Shop around before buying your red plates as they can be bought for the prices quoted below.

Blue and red sherbets and plates with the American Sweetheart SHAPE have appeared this year. Had they turned up with the design on them, collectors would have beaten a path to your door for the sherbets. As they are, they merely make an interesting addition to a collection of red or blue which heretofore was sans sherbets; in fact, they're even rather striking when contrasted with the monax.

Little of the black trimmed American Sweetheart referred to as "smoke" has come out of hiding. The plate at the back of the photograph is a pretty sample of "smoke". My only criteria for prices was what I paid for some. I would hope you'd find yours cheaper.

A few years ago monax (a milky white color) sugar lids could not be bought for any price; but their seeming scarcity has proved fallacious. So far, the price line is holding simply because many people refuse to sell at a lower price. Yet, there are at least a dozen other sugar lids more scarce than this one! Thus, because some sugar lids are worth so much more than the sugar bowl, I have priced them separately in this book.

Monax sherbets with a fired on red rim have been found along with green and orange fired on salver (11 - 12 inch serving plates).

Two new monax bowls have shown up. One is a smaller version of the 18 inch wide flanged (and rarely found) console bowl; the other is hat shaped.

This year pink shakers have edged ahead of monax in price. Numerous collectors are still seeking the monax; yet there are fewer pink to go around. The 9 ounce pink tumbler is rapidly disappearing from the market; grab them now.

American Sweetheart shakers have turned up in red (I've a snapshot), green and a peach colored "pink". The green is on the cover. The only problem with all these shakers is that the colors are fired on over pink glass and are not true colored glass.

Cups and saucers are available in cremax (a beige-like color); but there is little demand for them.

Cremax lampshades (two on floor lamps) have surfaced; yet, to my knowledge, only the one alabaster-like base with a shade has appeared. The shades do sometimes have orange, green, brown and blue panels over the design.

FLASH! The pink 4½" bud vase (a treasure!) shown on the opposite page is one of a kind and so recently discovered that special arrangements had to be made to get it included!

	PINK	MONAX	RED	BLUE	CREMAX	SMOKE
Bowl, 3¾", Flat, Berry	7.50				15.00	
Bowl, 4½", Cream Soup	7.50	27.50				
Bowl, 6" Cereal	2.25	5.00			6.50	12.50
Bowl, 9" Round, Berry	7.50	22.50			25.00	45.00
Bowl, 9½" Flat Soup	6.50	17.50				
Bowl, 11" Oval Vegetable	9.50	25.00				
Bowl, 18" Console		225.00	475.00	550.00		
Creamer, Footed	3.00	4.50	75.00	85.00		12.50
Cup	3.00	6.00	70.00	80.00		25.00
Lampshade					250.00	
Lamp (Complete)					700.00	
Plate, 6" Bread and Butter	1.00	2.50				8.00
Plate, 8" Salad	2.00	3.50	60.00	75.00		10.00
Plate, 9" Luncheon	2.50	4.75				12.50
Plate, 9¾"-10¼" Dinner	3.25	6.00				15.00
Plate, 11" Chop Plate	4.75	7.00				
Plate, 12" Salver	6.00	8.00	120.00	145.00		
Plate, 15½" Server		110.00	225.00	250.00		
Platter, 13" Oval	8.00	27.50				50.00
Pitcher, 7½", 60 oz.	160.00					
Pitcher, 8", 80 oz.	135.00					
*Salt and Pepper, Footed	125.00	115.00				
Saucer	1.50	2.00	27.50	32.50		10.00
Sherbet, Footed, 4"	6.50	10.00				
Sherbet, Footed, 4¼" (Design inside or outside)	2.75	5.00				
Sherbet in Metal Holder (Crystal Only) 3.00						
Sugar, Open, Footed	3.25	4.50	85.00	85.00		12.50
Sugar Cover (Monax Only)**		95.00				
Tidbit 2 Tier, 8" and 12"	25.00	50.00	250.00	250.00		
Tidbit 3 Tier, 8", 9" x 10¼"		60.00				
Tidbit 3 Tier, 8", 12" & 15½"		75.00	300.00	400.00		
Tumbler, 3½", 5 oz.	12.00					
*Tumbler, 4", 9 oz.	14.00					
Tumbler, 4½", 10 oz.	13.50					

*See green shaker on cover.
**Two style knobs.

ANNIVERSARY

(pink) (recently in crystal and iridescent)

JEANETTE GLASS COMPANY
1947-1949

The behind the scenes happenings in the rephotographing of this pattern make me believe that "anniversary" wished to be forgotten! First of all, a dish from another pattern got placed in the picture and it's only by the miracle of a photographer's technique called "air brushing" that you don't view it here. Secondly, I was tickled to find a wine glass to photograph this time. The reason you don't see it is because John Davis got so excited and involved in the discussion of ideas for the book that were bouncing about the room that he held the little wine glass in his hand the whole time the photographer was shooting. Thus, the wine glass is conspicuous in this third book only by its absence! Sorry! For those who don't know John, the only "spirits" involved were those of jocularity!)

The popularity of pink Anniversary has increased remarkably since the last book; but there seems to be little or no demand for crystal except for the butter dish and cover which should be priced about thirty per cent below the pink. The wine glass, 9 inch fruit bowl and the 12½" sandwich server are all getting to be tough pieces to find.

Anniversary was issued in the late 1940's instead of the 1930's; and, as such, it's really a sort of "cousin" to the true Depression era glassware. Remember, too, that the iridescent issue is from the early 1970's and should be very moderately priced. Don't be duped into buying it at overboard prices that some uninformed souls insist on placing on their "old" or so-called "carnival" glass.

Pink Anniversary makes an excellent beginning set to collect as it is still an inexpensive pattern and not everyone and his aunt is trying to collect a set as happens with some of the other patterns.

	CRYSTAL	PINK
Bowl, 4⅞" Berry	1.00	1.25
Bowl, 7⅜" Soup	2.50	3.00
Bowl, 9" Fruit	4.25	6.00
Butter Dish and Cover	20.00	30.00
Candy Jar and Cover	7.00	15.75
*Comport, Open, 3 Legged	2.00	2.00
Cake Plate, 12½"	5.00	6.00
Cake Plate with Cover	8.00	10.00
Creamer, Footed	2.50	3.00
Cup	2.00	2.50
Pickle Dish, 9"	3.50	3.75

	CRYSTAL	PINK
Plate, 6¼" Sherbet	1.00	1.25
Plate, 9" Dinner	2.25	3.00
Plate, 12½" Sandwich Server	4.00	5.00
Relish Dish, 8"	4.00	4.50
Saucer	1.00	1.25
Sherbet, Footed	2.00	3.00
Sugar	2.25	3.00
Sugar Covers	2.00	3.00
Vase, 6½"	5.00	8.50
Vase, Wall Pin-up	8.00	9.50
Wine Glass, 2½ oz.	3.00	7.50

*Old form; presently called compote.
Open compote or candy.

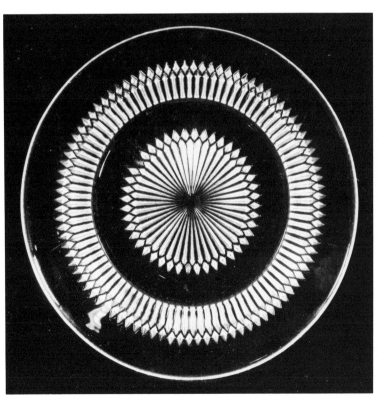

AUNT POLLY

(green, blue, iridescent)

JENKINS GLASS COMPANY
Late 1920's

Since its inclusion in the previous issue, the popularity of Aunt Polly has really grown. However, be sure to look closely at the pattern as there are several others with pieces of the same shape. The actual manufacturer is still enigmatic though the company is surely also the manufacturer of the Floral and Diamond and Strawberry patterns since the characteristics of those patterns are so similar to those of Aunt Polly.

Blue Aunt Polly has caught the fancy of many collectors and except for a few of the very plain Depression Glass patterns, it is the least expensive blue to collect. Coffee drinkers should be aware that this pattern has no cups and saucers; Floral and Diamond and Strawberry share a similar fate. Aunt Polly in blue is easier to find than in green; but the demand for blue keeps the prices higher. Shakers are difficult to find; thus it follows that shakers have made the biggest jump in price of any of the pieces in blue.

No pitchers or tumblers have turned up in green, nor have any shakers. There are numerous shakers similar to green Aunt Polly which would probably blend into a setting with no difficulty. However, most of these do not have the Aunt Polly diamond effect caused by crisscrossing swirls; rather they have swirls going only in one direction.

I am removing pink from the list of colors as I haven't been able to confirm a piece in that color.

Notice the additional listing of the 4¾ inch bowl in green. The bowl is two inches deep; and interestingly enough, it has a ground bottom, a characteristic commonly associated with older, better quality glassware than Depression is thought of as being. I lucked into this piece in Colorado; so not all unusual finds come out of the east!

	GREEN IRIDESCENT	BLUE
Bowl, 4⅜″ Berry	1.25	2.00
Bowl, 4¾″ 2″ High	7.00	7.00
Bowl, 7¼″ Oval, Handled Pickle	5.00	8.50
Bowl, 7⅞″ Large Berry	7.00	7.00
Bowl, 8⅜″ Oval	9.50	10.00
Butter Dish and Cover	100.00	75.00
Candy, Cover, Two Handled	8.00	12.50

	GREEN IRIDESCENT	BLUE
Creamer	5.00	8.00
Pitcher, 8″, 48 oz.		75.00
Plate, 6″ Sherbet	1.25	2.00
Plate, 8″ Luncheon		4.00
Salt and Pepper		100.00
Sherbet	4.50	5.50
Sugar	8.00	8.00
Sugar Cover	20.00	20.00
Tumbler, 3⅝″, 8 oz.		8.00
Vase, 6½″, Footed	12.00	12.00

Please refer to Foreword for pricing information

17

AVOCADO, "SWEET PEAR", No. 601

(pink, green, crystal)

INDIANA GLASS COMPANY
1923-1933

Collecting of Avocado has really slowed down, and it's a shame because it is one of the most interesting and readily recognizable patterns in Depression Glass. This slow down is mostly due, of course, to Tiara's again issuing pitcher and tumbler sets in the pattern beginning in August of 1973. Tiara Exclusive Home Products have since issued sets in pink, frosted pink, two shades of amber and amethyst and will probably issue some in green although their green is a much darker color than the one pictured here. The best advice I can give you as to how to know if you're getting an old pitcher and tumblers is to know your dealer or the glass. I might add that it may be a good idea for you to keep up with the Tiara representative in your area. This would clue you to the new products being issued and in what colors, not only in the Avocado pattern but in the other Indiana lines (such as Sandwich for which Indiana still has the old molds).

The older pink is very light in color, whereas the newer issued pink is darker and has a sort of orange cast to it. We purposely photographed an old and a new pink tumbler hoping to clearly show you the contrast that can be seen with the naked eye. However, picking up color on film is an "iffy" business at best and any difference to be seen here is negligible. The older tumbler is to the right near the pink plate in the picture.

The "rare page" of this book features the "apple" plate in amber; this shade of amber is different from either of the ambers produced by Tiara. I still can't confirm that Indiana made it, but it seems a good bet since it is so similar to the pears on the Avocado line. These amber plates have been found in Texas and in Indiana by collectors.

Tantalizingly, I've a report of a pitcher in milk glass; I've not yet seen it.

For the neophyte, saucers are harder to acquire than cups; and pitchers and tumblers are elusive in green.

I, personally, like the Avocado pattern and hope you will not write it off entirely. As long as you are careful of the pink pitcher and tumblers as well as any unusual colors, you should be safely purchasing older glassware.

	PINK	GREEN
Bowl, 5¼", Two-Handled	3.50	3.50
Bowl, 6" Relish, Footed	4.00	4.00
Bowl, 7" Preserve		
One Handle	3.50	3.50
Bowl, 7½" Salad	4.50	5.00
Bowl, 8" Oval, Two-Handled	5.00	5.00
Bowl, 8½" Berry	8.50	11.00
Bowl, 9½", 3¼" Deep	15.00	17.50
Creamer, Footed	10.00	10.00
Cup, Footed	7.00	8.00

*Caution on pink. The orangeish-pink is new!
**Apple Design $8.00. Amber $20.00.

	PINK	GREEN
*Pitcher, 64 ozs.	75.00	250.00
Plate, 6¼" Sherbet	2.00	2.00
**Plate, 8¼" Luncheon	3.00	4.00
Plate, 10¼"		
Two Handled Cake	10.00	12.50
Saucer	3.50	3.50
Sherbet	10.00	12.50
Sugar, Footed	10.00	10.00
*Tumbler	12.50	30.00

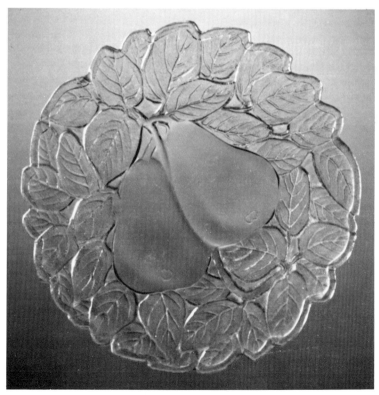

19

BEADED BLOCK

(pink, green, crystal, ice blue, vaseline, iridescent, amber, opalescent colors, and red)

IMPERIAL GLASS COMPANY 1927-1930's

Beaded Block is one of the patterns newly listed in this third edition. I trust it is quite obvious from the design how the name was arrived at for this; and this is good because it makes the pattern one of those which can be easily identified. Further, it is available in a veritable array of colors; so one should please you particularly. I only recently found a 6" lily bowl in red; and because someone told me they'd seen a piece in black, I spent an extra three hours combing a flea market trying to locate it, quite unsuccessfully, I might add. Either someone else spotted it, too; or the report was erroneous; for there was just no way I could have missed seeing it. So, look around. Especially desirable colors include vaseline, carnival, blue, red and those with opalescent shadings.

You may find additional pieces in the pattern as I have already found a few that weren't in the Imperial catalogue listing I studied. You will find variations in the sizes of pieces because this was hand worked glass and no matter how many times a person ruffles or flutes a piece of glass, he'll not do it exactly the same way twice; and when you get several people doing the handwork, then you get an even greater margin of variance. For this pattern, I have listed sizes according to the pieces I measured rather than what was on the catalogue listing when I found they varied from each other.

The ice blue color is represented in the picture by the two handled pickle dish and the one handled olive bowl. The iridized "carnival-like" bowl is Imperial's two handled jelly rather than our normally known cream soup. The pretty blue opalescent piece in the back is a bouquet vase rather than a parfait. The taller footed pieces in the back are Imperial's footed jelly dishes, not compotes; and the iridescent round bowl at center right is the lily bowl which I found in red.

I have seen a lily bowl in milk glass. However, it was marked inside with the dotted I G symbol which indicates it is newer made glassware.

You might like to notice how the square and round bowls were made by turning up the edges of the square and round plates.

This is one of those patterns that you often spot in antique shops flying the false colors of "carnival glass", "vaseline glass" or even "pattern" glass; due to its being hand worked, it is a better class glassware than what is usually termed Depression Glass. However, having been made during that era in the colors of the time, it may well be listed in the annals as Depression Glass.

	CRYSTAL*, PINK GREEN, AMBER	OTHER COLORS
Bowl, 4½", 2 handled jelly	3.50	10.00
**Bowl, 4½", round, lily	6.00	12.50
Bowl, 5½", square	3.50	6.00
Bowl, 5½", blue, 1 handle	4.00	7.50
Bowl, 6", deep, round	5.00	12.00
Bowl, 6¼", round	5.00	12.00
Bowl, 6½", round	5.00	12.00
Bowl, 6½", 2 handled pickle	6.50	13.00
Bowl, 6¾", round, unflared	6.00	11.00
Bowl, 7¼", round, flared	6.50	12.00
Bowl, 7½", round, fluted edges	10.00	15.00
Bowl, 7½", round, plain edge	6.50	10.00
Bowl, 8¼", celery	7.50	12.00
Creamer	7.50	12.50
Pitcher, 5¼", pint jug	25.00	40.00
Plate, 7¾", square	3.50	7.00
Plate, 8¾", round	3.50	7.00
Stemmed Jelly, 4½"	4.00	9.00
Stemmed Jelly, 4½", flared top	4.50	10.00
Vase, 6", bouquet	5.00	12.00

*All pieces except pitcher, 25% lower.
**Red: $40.00.

21

BLOCK OPTIC, "BLOCK"

(green, pink, yellow, crystal) **HOCKING GLASS COMPANY 1929-1933**

There were numerous block-like patterns issued during the Depression by other companies; thus, this is one of the harder to distinguish patterns for newcomers to the field. A couple of helps, aside from the picture, are that a number of the pieces have the same shape as do those of "Cameo", though there are other shapes; and most of the stemmed pieces have rayed bottoms. You might notice that the vase on the left is the same mold as the rare vase in Cameo. This one is even more rare.

To date, this pattern has been priced cheaply due both to accessibility and the lack of collectors buying it. This has changed somewhat in the past year. Although the price hasn't increased tremendously, it has increased in many of the harder to find items such as the yellow shakers and candy dish, or the green squatty shakers, mugs and tumble-ups (a jug with an inverted drinking glass serving as its top). Yellow is the most desirable color to own due to its general scarcity, of course.

Previously, I listed two styles of cups in Block Optic. However, it has been proven to me by several collectors that in reality there are four styles of cups based upon the shapes of the handles.

One major note is that the saucer and the sherbet plate are the same. There is no cup ring in the normally found saucer as is the case with several of Anchor Hocking patterns. I have heard rumors of a few saucers being found with cup rings but I have yet to see one.

I am removing the round butter dish from the listing in this pattern as there seem to be none around. I have followed up on close to fifty letters this year hoping to find one, yet nearly all have turned out to be the "Colonial Block" butter dish made by Hazel Atlas. The base of the Colonial Block will be marked with an H A which is the mark of the Hazel Atlas Glass Company. The reason Colonial Block isn't included in this book is due to the fact that only the butter dish, candy dish, creamer and sugar seem to exist and that's too few pieces to warrant a separate listing.

Crystal still has so few collectors that I haven't priced it separately. You should, therefore, be able to get it "for a song" as they say.

Price-wise, this is another pattern for beginning collectors. Yet, it may take some time to acquire an absolutely complete set.

	PINK, GREEN	YELLOW
Bowl, 4¼" Berry	1.00	
Bowl, 5¼" Cereal	1.50	3.50
Bowl, 7" Salad	3.50	4.50
Bowl, 8½" Large Berry	5.00	8.00
Butter Dish and Cover, 3" x 5"	*	12.50
Candlesticks, 1¾", Pr.	12.00	
Candy Jar and Cover, 2¼"	12.50	27.50
Candy Jar Cover, 6¼"	17.50	*
Comport, 4" Wide Mayonnaise	4.00	*
Creamer, Three Styles: Cone Shaped, Round Footed and Flat	2.75	4.00
Cup, Four Styles	2.00	3.00
Goblet, 4" Cocktail	4.50	*
Goblet, 4½", Wine	4.50	*
Goblet, 5¾", 9 oz.	6.00	*
Goblet, 7¼", Thin, 9 oz.	6.00	12.50
Ice Tub or Butter Tub, Open	7.50	*
Mug, Flat Creamer, No Spout	12.50	
Pitcher, 8½", 54 oz.	12.50	

	PINK, GREEN	YELLOW
Pitcher, 8", 80 oz.	15.00	
Plate, 6" Sherbet	1.00	1.25
Plate, 8" Luncheon	1.25	1.50
Plate, 9" Dinner	4.00	5.00
Plate, 9" Grill	2.50	*
Salt and Pepper, Footed	12.50	35.00
Salt and Pepper, Squatty	10.00	*
Sandwich Server, Center Handle	10.00	
Saucer (Same as sherbet plate)	1.00	1.25
Sherbet, Non Stemmed	1.25	2.00
Sherbet, 3¼", 5½ oz.	2.50	3.50
Sherbet, 4¾", 6 oz.	3.50	4.75
Sugar, Three Styles: As Creamer	2.75	4.00
Tumbler, 3½", 5 oz. Flat	2.00	*
Tumbler, 4", 5 oz. Footed	3.25	*
Tumbler, 9 oz. Flat	2.25	*
Tumbler, 9 oz. Footed	3.50	5.00
Tumbler, 10 oz. Flat	4.00	*
Tumbler, 6", 10 oz. Footed	4.25	5.75
Tumble-up Night Set: 3" Tumbler Bottle and Tumbler, 6" High	12.50	
Vase, 5¾", Blown	22.50	
Whiskey, 2½"	2.25	

Please refer to Foreword for pricing information

*Item should exist as listed in old catalogs or other publications but can not be confirmed by author.

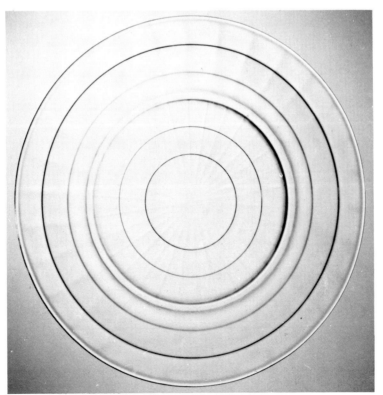

23

"BOWKNOT"

(green)

UNKNOWN MANUFACTURER

Probably late 1920's

We call this pattern by its "nickname" 'Bowknot' simply because its official name has not yet been proclaimed. One of these days someone is going to find an old catalogue listing or magazine advertisement giving its real "handle" and hopefully, listing the manufacturer. If that someone is you, I'd appreciate a post card!

Bowknot is a molded, heavy glass which is not to be confused with Fostoria's June pattern which is a thinner, better quality glassware that has a similar bow etched into the glass.

There are no new pieces to report so far; they still number only seven! I had hoped someone would discover a punch bowl or a little saucer somewhere to explain the presence of the cups. It seems odd to me to have cups only, but that is the way it is for now.

We also need to turn up a pitcher to go with the two styles of tumblers. Can't we pioneers of this field go forth and discover?

	GREEN
Bowl, 4½" Berry	1.00
Bowl, 5½" Cereal	1.50
Cup	2.00
Plate, 7" Salad	1.50

	GREEN
Sherbet, Low Footed	1.50
Tumbler, 5", 10 oz.	4.00
Tumbler, 5", 10 oz. Footed	7.00

25

"BUBBLE", "FIRE KING"

(pink, dark green, ruby red, crystal)

HOCKING GLASS COMPANY
1934-1965

Though "Bubble" is what collectors have dubbed this, it was first a pink bowl called "Bullseye" in 1934; then it was pale blue "Fire King" during the 1940's; with the issuing of the ruby red pitcher and tumblers in the mid 1960's, it got to be "Provincial". I suspect that no matter how it was christened, "Bubble" will head its epitaph.

In spite of previous laughs and poor relation snubbing by advanced collectors, blue and red Bubble is gaining in popularity all the time. A few collectors are beginning to buy the crystal, but so far they are so few that the crystal still commands only about half the price of the blue.

Creamers, soup bowls and platters in blue seem to be the most elusive.

That 8⅜ inch berry bowl in pink seems very plentiful. I know you'll be delighted to know that on my last trip to Hocking, I saw stacks and stacks of this bowl in pink and crystal still in the warehouses. A collector in California has also found a cup and saucer in pink; so the bowl is no longer the only piece to be found in pink.

Dark green candlesticks can be found in the Bubble pattern. I received a photograph of some with a label attached attributing these to Anchor Hocking.

The jadite (opaque green) bowl in the center was made in the 1950's; but I can't ascertain when the amber colored cup was made. Evidently, the amber pieces were short lived or experimental.

Notice these two styles of lamps. The one on the left was made by putting two candle holders together and applying feet to the bottom.

	DARK GREEN	LIGHT BLUE	RUBY RED
Bowl, 4" Berry		.75	1.00	
Bowl, 4½" Fruit	.85	1.25	1.75
Bowl, 5¼" Cereal	1.00	1.75	
Bowl, 7¾" Flat Soup	2.00	3.00	
Bowl, 8⅜" Large Berry (Pink—$2.50)	4.25	3.50	
Candlesticks (Crystal — $8.00 Pr.)	12.00		
Creamer	3.00	6.00	
*Cup	1.00	1.50	2.50
Lamp, 2 styles, Crystal Only — 15.00			
Pitcher, 64 oz., Ice Lip			15.00

	DARK GREEN	LIGHT BLUE	RUBY RED
Plate, 6¾" Bread and Butter	.75	1.00	
Plate, 9⅜" Grill		2.25	
Plate, 9⅜" Dinner	3.00	2.50	3.25
Platter, 12" Oval	3.00	4.00	
**Saucer	.75	1.00	1.50
Sugar	2.50	3.00	
Tidbit (2 Tier)			10.00
Tumbler, 6 oz. Juice			3.00
Tumbler, 9 oz. Water			3.50
Tumbler, 12 oz. Iced Tea			5.00
Tumbler, 16 oz. Lemonade			8.00

*Pink — $15.00.
**Pink — $2.00.

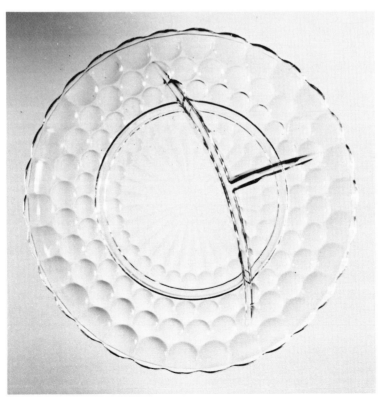

CAMEO, "BALLERINA," or "DANCING GIRL"

(green, yellow, pink and crystal with a platinum rim) **HOCKING GLASS COMPANY 1930-1934**

Even new collectors readily recognize Cameo pattern by the "dancing girl" figure. This is one of the top five most collected patterns in Depression Glass, the other four being Cherry Blossom, Mayfair, Miss America and Sharon. The problems with collecting Cameo are one, there are so many pieces that collecting "complete" sets get to be expensive; and two, this pattern has a number of one-of-a-kind items to date which you may always hope for and very possibly never find. However, if you can be content with getting just the basic pieces, it should be relatively easy to get a table setting capable of impressing your friends. The collection photographed at right is part of a $2000.00 investment. Tell that to your Aunt who sniffs and says she gave that old stuff to her cleaning lady!

New pieces of Cameo exposed from hiding include a new size wine (3½"), pictured next to the normal wine, and a new size iced tea, 6 3/8", 16 ounce. There are no new reports of square plates in yellow; I have heard of one in pink. A large pink berry bowl and a footed juice have turned up; however, those "two" pink ice bowls turned out to be one and the same---just two reports of it. Thus, the rarity of this item is "on ice", so to speak! The 4 3/4 inch vase or tumbler at the right of the cup and saucer is pictured here for the first time. At this writing, it is unique, also.

At least three completed Cameo butter dishes in yellow are now "together". You can see the bottom half of a potential one pictured.

More saucers with cup rings are appearing though they're still scarce; and since so many pink Cameo tumblers are showing up, surely it's only a matter of time until a pink pitcher falls out of the woodwork. If you get it, send me a picture!

The mystery of the odd lid hasn't been conclusively solved. It does fit the 6 inch rope edged juice pitcher, and one of the larger pitchers was found with a lid in an original box. Should you have further knowledge on the subject however, please inform us!

The "what's it" behind that flat soup on the lower right which looks like a large sherbet and which caused so much confusion previously is a mayonnaise.

Something not to "walk on by" next time you see it is crystal cameo with a platinum band. This is catching eyes since it's a bit more elegant with your good silver.

New collectors should know that the domino drip tray is called thus because it was made to hold the cream pitcher within the center ring surrounded by domino sugar cubes.

	GREEN	YELLOW	PINK	CRYS/PLAT
Bowl, 4¼" Sauce				3.50
Bowl, 4¾" Cream Soup	27.50			
Bowl, 5½" Cereal	5.50		7.50	3.00
Bowl, 7¼" Salad	7.50			
Bowl, 8¼" Large Berry	8.50	20.00		
Bowl, 9" Rimmed Soup	10.75			
Bowl, 10" Oval Vegetable	6.50	12.00		
Bowl, 11" 3 Leg Console	17.50	32.50	10.50	
Butter Dish and Cover	87.50	325.00		
Cake Plate, 10" 3 Legs	8.00			
Candlesticks, 4" Pr.	30.00			
Candy Jar, Low 4" and Cover	27.50	37.50		
Candy Jar, 6½" Tall and Cover	57.50	175.00		
Cocktail Shaker (Metal Lid) Appears in Crystal Only				125.00
Comport, 4" Wide, Mayonnaise	12.50			
Cookie Jar and Cover	16.00			
Creamer, 3¼"	7.50	5.00		
Creamer, 4¼"	6.50		32.50	
Cup, Two Styles	5.00	4.00	35.00	
Decanter, 10" With Stopper	35.00			
Decanter, 10" With Stopper, Frosted (Stoppers Represent ½ Value of Decanter)	17.00			
Domino Tray, 7" With 3" Indentation	35.00			
Domino Tray, 7" With No Indentation			125.00	
Goblet, 3½" Wine	40.00			
Goblet, 4" Wine	32.00		100.00	
Goblet, 6" Water	17.50		75.00	
Ice Bowl or Open Butter 3" Tall x 5½" Wide	72.50		300.00	
Jam Jar, 2" and Cover	57.50			

	GREEN	YELLOW	PINK	CRYS/PLAT
Pitcher, 5¾" Syrup or Milk, 20 oz.	97.50			
Pitcher, 6" Juice, 36 oz.	17.50			
Pitcher, 8½" Water, 56 oz.	17.50			
Plate, 6" Sherbet	1.50	1.50		1.50
Plate, 7" Salad				2.00
Plate, 8" Luncheon	2.00	1.75	17.00	3.00
Plate, 8½" Square	12.50	35.00		
Plate, 9½" Dinner	3.50	3.00	20.00	
Plate, 10" Sandwich	3.50		20.00	
Plate, 10½" Grill	3.00	2.50	22.50	
Plate, 10½" Grill With Closed Handles	3.00	2.50		
Plate, 10½" With Closed Handles	4.00	3.00		
Platter, 12", Closed Handles	5.00	5.00		
Relish, 3 Part, 7½" Footed	6.00	9.00		
Salt and Pepper, Footed, Pr.	27.50		375.00	
Sandwich Server, Center Handle	420.00			
Saucer With Cup Ring	20.00			
Saucer 6" (Sherbet Plate)	1.75	1.50		
Sherbet, 3⅛"	4.50	12.00	22.50	
Sherbet, 4⅞"	15.00	15.00	37.50	
Sugar, 3¼"	3.00	3.00		
Sugar, 4¼"	4.00		32.50	
Tumbler, 3¾", 5 oz. Juice	11.50		45.00	
Tumbler, 4", 9 oz. Water	9.00		45.00	5.50
Tumbler, 4¾", 10 oz. Flat	10.00			
Tumbler, 5", 11 oz. Flat	10.00	21.50		
Tumbler, 3 oz. Footed, Juice	30.00			
Tumbler, 5", 9 oz. Footed	7.50	6.75		
Tumbler, 5¾", 11 oz. Footed	15.00			
Tumbler, 6⅜", 15 oz. Footed	100.00			
Vase, 5¾"	62.50			
Vase, 8"	10.00			
Water Bottle (Dark Green) Whitehouse Vinegar	12.00			

Please refer to Foreword for pricing information

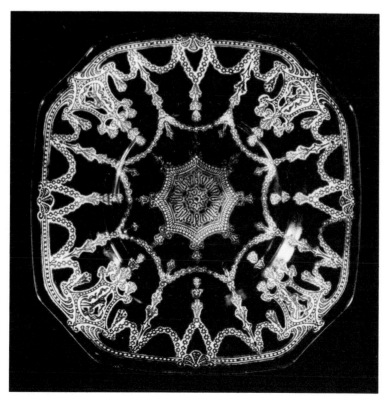

29

CHERRY BLOSSOM

(pink, green, delphite (opaque blue), crystal, jadite (opaque green), red

JEANETTE GLASS COMPANY 1930-1939

Cherry Blossom, one of the top five most collected patterns, is abundant and easily recognized by the cherries in the design. It is usually found in pink or green, those other colors mentioned being rather happenstance.

Major finds in this pattern since my last book include three 9" oval platters in delicate pink on which the creamer and sugar rest; two divided relish trays in an orange cast pink, patterned after the two handled, round, 10½" sandwich tray; two sets of PINK CHERRY SHAKERS, the transparent red cherry bowl featured on the cover; and a translucent apple green colored plate which really takes on "fire" when held to light. I will have it displayed at the shows I attend; so drop by and check it out with some other oddities. (Notice, also, on the cover the amber (?) child's cup and saucer. The question is there because it was either experimental amber or someone mixed up an awful batch of pink at the factory. Anyway, it's unusual.)

Initial collectors should note from the price list that children's mugs, butter dishes and child's dishes are desirable pieces to own. The last items are quite plentiful when compared with the supply of mugs.

I feel I should reiterate previous material concerning the 1973 production of "new pieces" in Cherry which caused havoc before the various depression publications (listed in the back of the book) could pour on the soothing oils of enlightenment. First came a child's cup with slightly lop-sided handles and the cherries hanging upside down when you held the cup in the right hand. (This was due to the inversion of the design when the mold, taken from an original cup, was inverted to create the outside of the "new" cup.) Once this was reported, this oddity was corrected after a fashion by re-inverting the inverted mold. There were also saucers with the designs slightly off center. Then came a deluge of a heretofore unmade item, a child's butter dish, ingeniously made by leaving off the handle from the child's cherry cups, turning the remaining bowl upside down on a saucer and adding a knob on top. It wobbled a little, but it was cute. The problem came when the obvious fact that all this was new was somehow lost and people got "taken". Hence, one of the inestimable values of keeping up via trade publications of what is happening in the world of Depression Glass. Ultimately, a cobalt blue, a grayish green and a marigold irridescent carnival child's butter turned up. Should you desire this novelty item, don't pay a lot for it as they were offered to dealers by the box load.

The letters AOP in the price listing refer to pieces having an "all over pattern"; PAT means "pattern at the top" only.

	PINK	GREEN	DELPHITE	JADITE		PINK	GREEN	DELPHITE
Bowl, 4¾" Berry	4.00	5.00	7.50		Plate, 9" Grill	7.00	7.00	
Bowl, 5¾" Cereal	7.50	9.00			Plate, 10" Grill	8.00	8.00	
Bowl, 7¾" Flat Soup	15.50	20.00			Platter, 9" Oval	300.00		
*Bowl, 8½" Round Berry	6.75	11.00	35.00		Platter, 11" Oval	12.50	13.00	27.50
Bowl, 9" Oval Vegetable	7.50	10.00	35.00		Platter, 13" and 13" Divided	17.50	20.00	
Bowl, 9" 2 Handled	7.00	10.00	10.00	200.00	Salt and Pepper			
Bowl, 10½", 3 Leg Fruit	17.50	21.00		200.00	Scalloped Bottom	1000.00	675.00	1000.00
Butter Dish and Cover	50.00	60.00			Saucer	2.00	2.50	4.00
Cake Plate (3 Legs) 10¼"	9.00	12.50			Sherbet	6.00	7.00	
Coaster	5.00	6.00			Sugar	6.00	7.00	15.00
Creamer	5.00	7.00	15.00		Sugar Cover	3.50	4.50	
Cup	8.00	9.00	11.00		Tray, 10½" Sandwich	7.00	10.00	12.75
Mug, 7 oz.	72.50	82.50			Tumbler, 3¾", 4 oz. Footed,			
Pitcher, 6¾" AOP, 36 oz.					AOP, Round or Scalloped	10.00	10.00	15.00
Scalloped or Round Bottom	22.50	27.50	87.50		Tumbler, 4½", 9 oz. Round			
Pitcher, 8" PAT, 36 oz. Flat	20.00	20.50			Foot AOP	17.50	20.00	16.00
Pitcher, 8" PAT, 42 oz. Flat	20.00	22.50			Tumbler, 4½", 8 oz.			
Pitcher, 8" PAT, 36 oz. Footed	20.00	22.50			Scalloped Foot AOP	17.50	20.00	16.00
Plate, 6" Sherbet (design on top)	3.00	3.00	8.00		Tumbler, 3½", 4 oz. Flat PAT	5.00	7.00	
Plate, 7" Salad	7.00	7.00			Tumbler, 4¼", 9 oz. Flat PAT	7.00	8.00	
**Plate, 9" Dinner	5.00	7.00	10.00		Tumbler, 5", 12 oz. Flat PAT	15.00	20.00	

*Yellow — $300.00. Red — $300.00.
**Translucent Green — $100.00.

Cherry Blossom — Child's Junior Dinner Set

	PINK	DELPHITE		PINK	DELPHITE
Creamer	17.50	22.50	Plate, 6" Design on Bottom	7.00	8.00
Sugar	17.50	22.50	Cup	13.00	20.00
Original box sells for $7.50 extra with these sets.			Saucer	4.50	5.00
			14 Piece Set	135.00	165.00

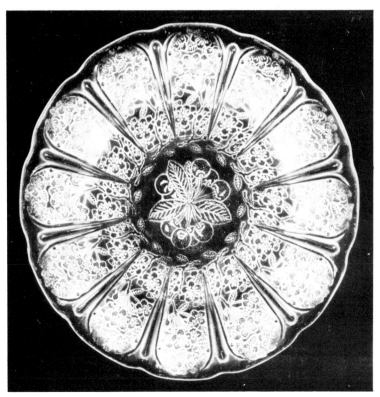

CHINEX CLASSIC

(ivory, ivory decorated)

MACBETH-EVANS DIVISION OF CORNING GLASS WORKS

Late 1930 - Early 1940

Chinex is collected by custard glass devotees as well as people interested in Depression Glass and I hope they all appreciate the photograph in color this time instead of the black and white.

As you can see, there are several different fired under glaze decals in this glassware as well as what is known as the "brown castle" design. This last design is generally the one most desired by collectors.

The shaded items pictured are more difficult to find than the plain ivory ones.

Sherbets and soup bowls in any design, as I previously warned, took lessons in concealment and are next to impossible to accumu-

late. In point of fact, none of this type glassware is overly plentiful. So if you run across a butter dish with a castle motif, don't snub it; you and only a handful of others will have one.

For a while, prices for this shot way up; now, they have leveled off at a more reasonable level for the number of people now collecting it. Should more collectors enter the field, no doubt the prices will resume their upward trend as, again, there just isn't that much of it to be found.

Note the scroll-like design on the plate as compared to the plainer Cremax discussed later.

	BROWNTONE OR PLAIN IVORY	DECAL DECORATED*
Bowl, 5¾" Cereal	3.25	4.00
Bowl, 7" Flat Soup	5.00	6.00
Bowl, 9" Vegetable	10.00	12.00
Butter Dish	52.50	75.00
Creamer	5.00	7.00
Cup	3.50	4.00
Plate, 6¼" Sherbet	2.00	2.00
Plate, 9¾" Dinner	3.50	4.50
Plate, 11½" Sandwich or Cake	7.00	7.50
Saucer	2.00	3.00
Sherbet, Low Footed	7.50	8.00
Sugar, Open	5.00	7.00

*Castle decal about 20% higher in most areas.

Please refer to Foreword for pricing information

CLOVERLEAF

(pink, green, yellow, crystal, black)

HAZEL ATLAS GLASS COMPANY

1930-1936

So far, Cloverleaf collectors have had the "good luck" to be in the minority. If many collectors should join this bandwagon, there simply would not be enough pieces to go around. In my many miles of traveling, I have found this pattern very scarce in almost all pieces except creamers and sugars.

Shakers in pink simply do not exist to my knowledge; so you will have to consider that price listing for the green color only.

The clever-at-hiding yellow candy dishes and shakers have taken big jumps in prices with the yellow shakers out jumping the black ones for now. Collectors are bemoaning the fact that small bowls in yellow are all but nonexistent.

Black sherbet plates are holding their own in price. Novice collectors should know that the sherbet plate and the saucer are the same size; yet the center of the saucer is plain while the sherbet plate has the cloverleaf design at its center.

In recent months several small black ash trays (an unknown item until my first book) have magically appeared; thus the larger black one is turning out to be the more difficult to possess even though it was the first discovered.

	PINK GREEN	YELLOW	BLACK
Ash Tray 4", Match Holder in Center			32.50
Ash Tray 5¾", Match Holder in Center			55.00
Bowl, 4" Dessert	3.25	9.00	
Bowl, 5" Cereal	4.50	9.00	
Bowl, 7" Salad	4.50	10.00	
Bowl, 8" Deep Bowl	9.00	15.00	
Candy Dish and Cover	**20.00	75.00	*
Creamer, Footed, 3⅝"	3.00	6.25	6.50
Cup	2.00	4.50	5.50
Plate, 6" Sherbet	1.25	3.00	15.00
Plate, 8" Luncheon	1.75	7.50	6.50
Plate, 10¼" Grill	2.75	6.75	
Salt and Pepper, Pair	**12.50	70.00	40.00
Saucer	1.00	2.00	2.25
Sherbet, 3" Footed	2.00	5.00	9.50
Sugar, Footed, 3⅝"	3.00	6.25	6.50
Tumbler, 4", 9 oz. Flat	5.50	*	
Tumbler, 3¾", 10 oz. Flat	7.50	*	
Tumbler, 5¾", 10 oz. Footed	7.75	12.50	

Design highlighted in photographs to emphasize pattern.

**Green only.

Please refer to Foreword for pricing information

*Item should exist as listed in old catalogs or other publications but can not be confirmed by author.

COLONIAL, "KNIFE AND FORK"

(pink, green, crystal, opaque white) **HOCKING GLASS COMPANY 1934-1938**

This Colonial pattern is a good one to collect, evidenced by its numerous collectors and its variety of pieces. It has a simple design which manages to exude a quiet elegance at the table or in the china cabinet. Even its name is rather picturesque and fetching in these times.

I trust you will settle for the old picture which I didn't really feel could be improved upon, particularly since only one new item has entered this sphere of collection. A pink pitcher with a beaded top instead of the plainer banded one (pictured) has turned up. It is otherwise patterned like the regular Colonial pitcher.

It would seem that there just aren't many pink Colonial butter dishes left in mint condition or otherwise. The few that have appeared have all been dinged or chunked up quite a lot. Butter tops in this pattern are quite heavy; so perhaps that explains some of the apparent shortage not only of pink butter dishes but of butter bottoms in general.

Prices have jumped in green dinner plates and in soup bowls, cream soups and spooners of all colors. The spooner is taller than the sugar bowl and the handles, thus, are higher up on the spooner.

Have you seen any pink cream soups? I haven't spotted any, but perhaps I'm just looking in the wrong places.

A white, Colonial-like luncheon plate has been uncovered to go with the white cup and saucer. However, it has concentric rings on it similar to those of Chinex and as such may have been produced by the Corning glassworks. Anyway, for those of you with white cups and saucers, here's your chance to serve dinner on your collection instead of just bridge party coffees.

Crystal Colonial is growing in popularity, but it still lags behind pink and green Colonial in price except for the spooner, which sells slightly lower than the green; and the shakers, which are holding steady at about $40. The remaining pieces in crystal run ten to fifteen per cent less than whichever price is lower in the green and pink list. Because of the price differential, crystal Colonial might be given serious consideration by new arrivals to the mania of collecting Depression Glass who are stymied by the prices of some patterns.

There seems to be a size differential on the tops for the wooden cheese boards and the regular butter dish which appeared to be one and the same. The top which best fits the cheese board is not as tall as the regular butter by about half an inch. (I note that fact for the purist; I really wouldn't be upset by your butter lid being atop your cheese board!)

I would recommend your collecting a certain size of stemware rather than all sizes unless your pocketbook goes to unlimited depths.

	PINK	GREEN		PINK	GREEN
Bowl, 4" Berry	2.00	4.50	Plate, 6" Sherbet	1.25	1.50
Bowl, 5½" Cereal	5.00	10.00	Plate, 8½" Luncheon	2.00	2.25
Bowl, 4½" Cream Soup	*	15.00	Plate, 10" Dinner	4.50	12.50
Bowl, 7" Low Soup	8.00	17.50	Plate, 10" Grill	3.00	6.25
Bowl, 9" Large Berry	7.00	8.50	Platter, 12" Oval	5.00	6.00
Bowl, 10" Oval Vegetable	8.00	11.00	Salt and Pepper, Pair	80.00	80.00
Butter Dish and Cover	285.00	27.50	Saucer (White 3.00)		
Cheese Dish (as shown)		50.00	(Same as sherbet plate)	1.25	1.50
Creamer, 5", 8 oz.			Sherbet	2.50	5.00
(Milk Pitcher)	7.00	9.00	Spoon Holder or Celery	25.00	27.50
Cup (White 7.00)	3.00	3.50	Sugar, 5"	7.00	7.00
Goblet, 3¾", 1 oz. Cordial	*	13.50	Sugar Cover	9.00	6.00
Goblet, 4" 3 oz. Cocktail	*	11.00	Tumbler, 3", 5 oz. Juice	5.00	8.00
Goblet, 4½", 2½ oz. Wine	10.00	12.50	Tumbler, 4", 9 oz. Water	4.00	10.00
Goblet, 5¼", 4 oz. Claret	*	9.00	Tumbler, 10 oz.	4.00	12.00
Goblet, 5¾", 8½ oz. Water	*	10.00	Tumbler, 12 oz. Iced Tea	6.50	13.50
Pitcher, 7", 54 oz.			Tumbler, 15 oz. Lemonade	10.00	17.50
Ice Lip or None	22.50	20.00	Tumbler, 3¼", 3 oz. Footed	5.25	8.00
**Pitcher, 7¾", 68 oz.			Tumbler, 4", 5 oz. Footed	6.50	9.50
Ice Lip or None	27.50	22.50	Tumbler, 5¼", 10 oz. Ftd.	7.50	11.50
			Whiskey, 2½", 1½ oz.	4.50	5.50

**Beaded top in pink $100.00.

*Item should exist as listed in old catalogs or
other publications but can not be confirmed
by author.

Please refer to Foreword for pricing information

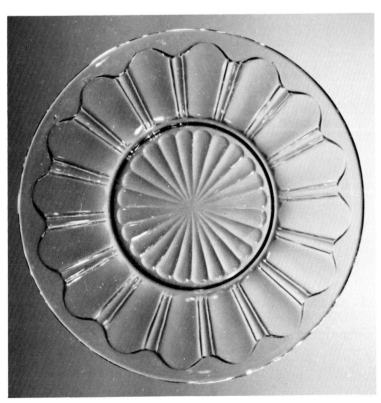

COLONIAL FLUTED, "ROPE"

(green, crystal)

FEDERAL GLASS COMPANY

1928-1933

Colonial Fluted was supposed to have been made in pink; but in all my travels, I've never seen a piece; so this time I'm not even listing that color.

The Federal mark is an "F" enclosed by a shield. Should you decide to collect this pattern of few pieces, my wish for you is that you see a lot of that mark. However, I have my doubts; for there are two basic problems with this pattern. One is simply finding it at all and the second is finding it in an acceptable condition. Most of the pieces that do turn up are badly scratched. They are seldom chipped, so the glass must be durable; the few pieces that exist must just have been used a lot.

There is a crystal bridge set in this that is a worthy find if you can get one without the hearts, diamonds, clubs and spades worn off. So keep an eye peeled for this whether you collect the pattern per se or not.

	GREEN		GREEN
Bowl, 4" Berry	1.00	Plate, 6" Sherbet	.75
Bowl, 6" Cereal	1.25	Plate, 8" Luncheon	1.00
Bowl, 6½" Deep Salad	3.00	Saucer	.75
Bowl, 7½" Large Berry	4.00	Sherbet	2.00
Creamer	2.25	Sugar	2.25
Cup	1.50	Sugar Cover	2.00

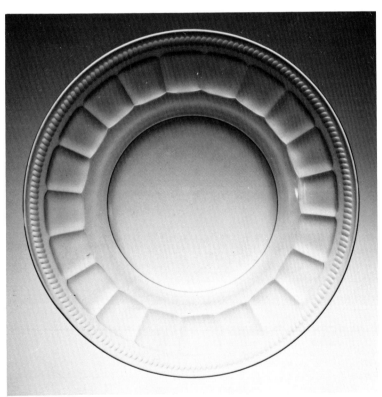

39

COLUMBIA

(crystal, pink)

FEDERAL GLASS COMPANY
1938-1942

You will find Columbia in crystal a great deal more than in pink. In fact, one of the items that many collectors would give their eye teeth for would be a butter dish in pink Columbia. Pink pieces of any kind are not easy to locate, but pink saucers are extremely tough to run into!

Quite a few different flashed colored butter tops have found their way into Columbia collections. You may see them in blue, iridescent, red, purple or even green. There may be other colors as well. Butters can be found sporting a metal lid; evidently these are original though they are not nearly so attractive as the glass.

Notice the crystal Columbia with the applied flower decals. This was probably not factory designed, but it does add something to the piece.

	CRYSTAL		CRYSTAL	PINK
Bowl, 5″ Cereal	1.00	Cup	1.50	4.50
Bowl, 8″ Low Soup	2.00	Plate, 6″ Bread & Butter	.75	2.50
Bowl, 8½″ Salad	4.00	Plate, 9½″ Luncheon	1.50	5.50
Bowl, 10½″ Ruffled Edge	7.00	Plate, 11¾″ Chop	4.00	
Butter Dish and Cover		Saucer	.75	2.50
Ruby Flashed (15.00)	10.00	Snack Plate	2.50	
Flashed (12.50)				

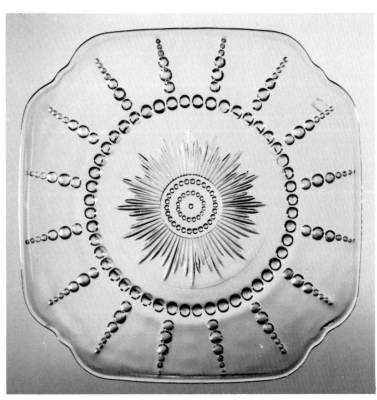

41

CORONATION, "BANDED FINE RIB", "SAXON"

(pink, crystal, ruby red)

HOCKING GLASS COMPANY
1936-1940

Ruby red Coronation berry sets exist in abundance. These were either extremely well promoted or the supply just exceeds the demand for them at present. However, Ruby saucers aren't to be found; thus you see red cups on crystal saucers at present which really doesn't look bad.

As is the case with most Hocking patterns, there is no cup ring on the saucer; thus the sherbet plate and the saucer are the same.

The Coronation tumbler causes a headache for some because it is so similar to the much rarer Lace Edge tumbler. The more plentiful Coronation tumbler has the fine rays going almost to the top of the glass whereas those of Lace Edge do not. Since they're so similar, of course, whichever you find will blend with your table setting. Dealers are concerned because of the price differential.

	PINK	RUBY RED		PINK	RUBY RED
Bowl, 4¼" Berry	1.00	2.25	Plate, 8½" Luncheon	1.50	2.75
Bowl, 6½" Nappy	1.25	5.00	Saucer	.75	
Bowl, 8" Large Berry	2.50	8.25	Sherbet	1.25	2.50
Cup	1.25	2.50	Tumbler, 5", 10 oz. Footed	4.00	
Plate, 6" Sherbet	.75				

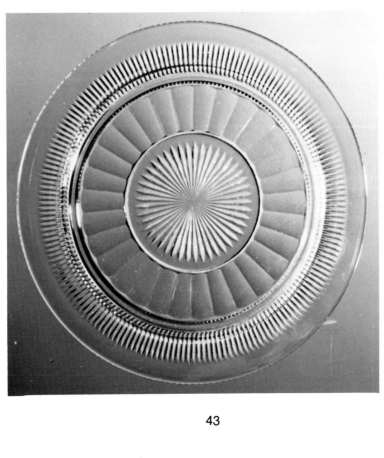

43

CREMAX

(cremax)

MACBETH-EVANS DIVISION OF CORNING GLASS WORKS

Late 1930's - Early 1940's

The basic difference between Cremax and Chinex is that Cremax doesn't have the scroll-like design of Chinex. The word "cremax" will be used to describe an off-white color found in American Sweetheart, Dogwood and Petalware which are other patterns put out by the Macbeth-Evans company but not by the Corning Division. In Cremax **pattern**, however, this color distinction isn't relevant. It's mostly as white as Chinex. Again, the difference between the two lies in the scroll-like design on the Chinex pieces.

Now, having said that, let me further confuse you by saying that the pie crust edged butter bottom you will find belongs to Chinex and not to Cremax. So far, a Cremax butter has not turned up. The Chinex scroll design is found only on the lid and not on the base of the butter. Thus, when people find the butter bottom without the top, they naturally assume it to be Cremax. If you should find a pie crust edged butter top that is otherwise plain and if it should fit the pie crust edged butter bottom, then we might assume that the two are interchangeable; however, since those conditions have not been met, then we must call the butter a Chinex butter for the time being.

Though you generally find a more colorful variety of decals decorating the Cremax than the Chinex, a number are the very same. Here, again, the castle decal is the most popular with collectors.

	CREMAX	DECAL DECORATED		CREMAX	DECAL DECORATED
Bowl, 5¾" Cereal	2.25	3.00	Plate, 9¾" Dinner	4.50	5.00
Bowl, 9" Vegetable	7.00	8.50	Plate, 11½" Sandwich	6.00	7.00
Creamer	3.00	3.25	Saucer	1.00	1.50
Cup	2.50	3.00	Sugar, Open	3.00	3.25
Plate, 6¼" Bread and Butter	1.75	2.00			

Please refer to Foreword for pricing information

CUBE, "CUBIST"

(pink, green, crystal, ultra-marine)

**JEANETTE GLASS COMPANY
1929-1933**

Unfortunately, no new pieces in Cube have shown up in the ultra-marine color; that bowl in the picture is the only one so far though I would bet that somebody out there has little bowls like it stashed in a cupboard.

The Cube pitcher first shown in this book has gradually creeped up in price with the green becoming the more difficult to run across. Green Cube tumblers have all but disappeared. Since green is in such short supply in any piece, most collecting is done in pink.

I have omitted the tray for the creamer and sugar from the listing as it appears only to occur in crystal. I'll be delighted for you to prove me wrong!

There are few collectors for crystal Cube; but beginning collectors who are considering doing that should be warned that the Fostoria Glass Company's "American" pattern is very similar to Cube; yet if you have the opportunity to compare them. You will find it to be a better quality glass of greater clarity than Jeanette's Cube.

	PINK	GREEN
Bowl, 4½" Dessert	1.50	1.75
Bowl, 4½" Deep	1.50	2.00
*Bowl, 6½" Salad	3.00	4.50
Butter Dish and Cover	30.00	32.50
Candy Jar and Cover, 6½"	13.50	15.00
Coaster, 3¼"	2.00	2.25
Creamer, 2"	1.50	
Creamer, 3"	2.25	3.50
Cup	2.25	2.75
Pitcher, 8¾", 45 oz.	60.00	90.00
Plate, 6" Sherbet	1.00	1.00

*Ultra-Marine — $20.00.

	PINK	GREEN
Plate, 8" Luncheon	1.75	2.00
Powder Jar and Cover, 3 Legs	8.00	9.50
Salt and Pepper, Pr.	12.00	15.00
Saucer	.75	.75
Sherbet, Footed	2.50	3.00
Sugar, 2"	1.50	
Sugar, 3"	2.25	3.50
Sugar/Candy Cover	3.00	4.00
Tray for 3" Creamer and Sugar, 7½" (crystal only)	3.00	
Tumbler, 4", 9 oz.	6.00	15.00

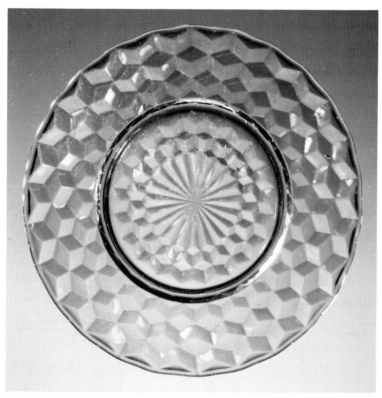

47

"DAISY", NUMBER 620

(crystal, 1933; amber, 1940; dark green and milk glass, 1960's)

INDIANA GLASS COMPANY

Indiana issued much of its glass under a number rather than a name. The naming of the pattern has come from collectors. The more recent issues of dark green and milk glass colors were called "Heritage" by the company. Depression Glass people continue to group it all under the heading "Daisy".

Several buyers in my area have discovered this little Daisy is not as plentiful as they thought. They are having particular difficulty in locating the taller footed tumbler, the 9⅜ inch berry bowl and the sherbets. If you have any of these pieces, consider yourself fortunate!

There is little demand for crystal Daisy as yet with the exception of gold or platinum trimmed pieces.

This makes an attractive setting; so don't take it too lightly; besides, it is an opportunity to have "daisys" on your table all year long!

	CRYSTAL	AMBER
Bowl, 4½" Berry	.50	1.00
Bowl, 4½" Cream Soup	1.50	3.00
Bowl, 6" Cereal	1.00	1.50
Bowl, 7⅜" Deep Berry	2.75	4.00
Bowl, 9⅜" Deep Berry	3.00	5.00
Bowl, 10" Oval Vegetable	2.50	5.00
Creamer, Footed	2.00	2.50
Cup	1.25	1.50
Plate, 6" Sherbet	.75	1.00
Plate, 7⅜" Salad	1.00	1.50
Plate, 8⅜" Luncheon	1.25	2.00

	CRYSTAL	AMBER
Plate, 9⅜" Dinner	1.75	2.75
Plate, 10⅜" Grill	1.25	2.25
Plate, 11½" Cake or Sandwich	2.00	3.75
Platter, 10¾"	4.00	6.00
Relish Dish, 3 Part, 8⅜"	2.00	3.50
Saucer	.75	1.00
Sherbet, Footed	1.50	2.25
Sugar, Footed	2.00	2.50
Tumbler, 9 oz. Footed	2.50	4.25
Tumbler, 12 oz. Footed	4.00	8.00

49

DIAMOND QUILTED, "FLAT DIAMOND"

(pink, blue, green, crystal, black)

IMPERIAL GLASS COMPANY
Late 1920's - Early 1930's

There were numerous diamond patterns made, but Imperial's diamonds were very flat and thus the nickname "flat diamond". Demand for a pattern, no matter how scarce it is, is the main factor in scooting up the prices. Diamond Quilted is fairly difficult to find, especially in blue and black; but there isn't a big demand for it, yet. So, here is an opportunity for you to get to "quilting" before everyone else starts grabbing the diamond patches.

I have only seen one black Diamond Quilted ice bucket and that was in Michigan. By the way, on the dark pieces, you have to look on the inside of the piece to find the diamonds as they won't "show through" the glass like they do in the transparent colors. The black pieces appear perfectly smooth on the outside. The blue ice bucket pictured came from Tennessee and was identical in mold to the black.

The amber color was either a short line or experimental. I have only seen the creamer, sugar, cup and saucer in it.

Wouldn't the rolled edge console bowl pictured in green be equally terrific in blue?

Several pieces of red including cups, creamers and sugars have been reported to me, but I haven't seen one. Keep looking around out there! We've still more to find!

	PINK, GREEN	BLUE, BLACK		PINK, GREEN	BLUE, BLACK
Bowl, 4¾" Cream Soup	3.25	8.00	Mayonnaise Set: Ladle,		
Bowl, 5" Cereal	1.50	3.50	Plate, 3 Footed Dish	9.00	
Bowl, 5½", One Handle	3.50	7.50	Pitcher, 64 oz.	15.00	
Bowl, 7" Crimped Edge	4.00	9.00	Plate, 6" Sherbet	1.00	2.75
Bowl, Rolled Edge Console	10.00	15.00	Plate, 7" Salad	1.25	3.50
Cake Salver, Tall 10"			Plate, 8" Luncheon	2.00	6.50
Diameter	20.00		Plate, 14" Sandwich	4.50	
Candlesticks (2 Styles) Pr.	7.00	15.00	Sandwich Server,		
Candy Jar and Cover, Ftd.	7.50	13.00	Center Handle	8.00	17.50
Compote and Cover, 11½"	25.00		Saucer	1.00	2.00
Creamer	3.00	7.50	Sherbet	2.25	6.00
Cup	1.75	4.00	Sugar	3.00	7.50
Goblet, 1 oz. Cordial	3.50		Tumbler, 9 oz. Water	3.25	
Goblet, 2 oz. Wine	3.50		Tumbler, 12 oz. Iced Tea	3.75	
Goblet, 3 oz. Wine	4.50		Tumbler, 6 oz. Footed	3.25	
Goblet, 6" 9 oz.			Tumbler, 9 oz. Footed	5.00	
Champagne	5.50		Tumbler, 12 oz. Footed	5.50	
Ice Bucket		32.50	Whiskey, 1½ oz.	3.50	

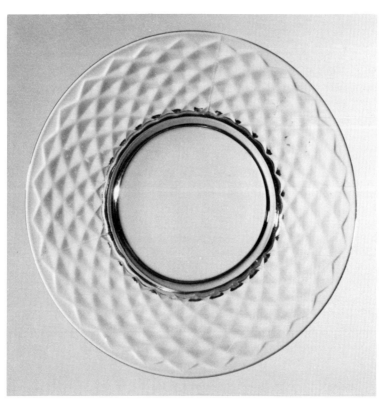

DIANA

(pink, amber, crystal)

FEDERAL GLASS COMPANY
1937-1941

Diana is one of the swirled Depression Glass patterns which tends to confuse some people. One of the best ways I've found to tell whether the piece I've found is Diana or not is to notice if the bottom of the item is swirled also. If it is, then it's Diana. Perhaps a story line will fix the pattern in your mind. You remember that Diana of mythology was the goddess of the moon; when you look at this glass just right, you get a fleeting illusion of the moon and its shimmery light.

All my life I've been told that fishing is mostly skill and very little luck. Well, a skillful Depression angler has hooked an amber shaker! Lucky duck! At least my prediction last time that skilled fishing would hook one has come true. Another hard to find item in amber is the candy dish; so don't overlook it.

The frosted large bowl in the back of the photo is not one of the prettiest pieces I've ever seen, but it is unusual. A complete set of frosted pink Diana surfaced early this spring; so Federal must have dipped some of this pattern in camphoric acid at one time. Generally, the frosted items bring less than the regular issue because of little demand for it.

Demitasse cup and saucer sets in pink Diana are sometimes found on a rack like the one pictured with the crystal set.

A few earlier made items with Diana characteristics can be found in green such as the newly listed sherbet and the ash tray coaster shown in the lower right corner.

	AMBER, CRYSTAL, PINK
*Ash Tray, 3½"	2.00
Bowl, 5" Cereal	1.50
Bowl, 5½" Cream Soup	4.00
Bowl, 9" Salad	4.50
Bowl, 11" Console Fruit	5.25
Bowl, 12" Scalloped Edge	6.00
**Candy Jar and Cover, Round	10.00
Coaster, 3½"	2.00
Creamer, Oval	3.00
Cup	2.25
Cup, Demi-tasse, 2 oz. and 4½" Saucer Set	3.00

	AMBER, CRYSTAL, PINK
Plate, 5½" Child's	2.00
Plate, 6" Bread and Butter	1.25
Plate, 9½" Dinner	2.75
Plate, 11¾" Sandwich	3.00
Platter, 12" Oval	4.00
***Salt and Pepper, Pr.	20.00
Saucer	1.00
Sherbet	3.00
Sugar, Open, Oval	3.00
Tumbler, 4⅛", 9 oz.	7.00
Junior Set: 6 Cups, Saucer and Plates with Round Rack	30.00

Please refer to Foreword for pricing information

*Green — $3.00
**Amber — $15.00
***Amber — $50.00

DOGWOOD, "APPLE BLOSSOM", "WILD ROSE"

(pink, green, crystal, monax, cremax and yellow) **MACBETH-EVANS GLASS COMPANY 1929-1932**

The decorative flowers you see on the Dogwood pitcher, tumblers and the little five ounce juice glass (shown for the first book skeptics who couldn't believe it existed) were painted on by silk screen process. Again, I have only included the decorated pieces in my listing though plain pitchers and tumblers do exist. My reasoning for this is that the same styles exist in "S" pattern. So who's to know if you have a plain Dogwood pitcher without the Dogwoods or a plain "S" pitcher without the "S" pattern. We know that Macbeth-Evans sold the plain ones; and Dogwood collectors will settle for them to complete a set when they absolutely can't find anything else; but they much prefer the decorated items to the plain.

Dogwood is another pattern in which the supply of pink is far above that of green. That luncheon plate in pink is the most commonly found item; however, the larger dinner plate is a really tough item to acquire. You will note a jump in prices of the really hard to find pink pieces. Oh, for that day in Ohio when I bought four pink platters and left two sitting that had small nicks! I'm lucky to **see** four a year, now! The large pink fruit bowl, which measures 10¼ inches rather than the 9½ inches I listed, has caught up with the green Dogwood in price more by demand than for its scarcity.

Green Dogwood has always been more difficult to put together a set in and prices keep mirroring this fact. Several more green Dogwood pitchers and large green bowls have arrived on the scene, but they aren't exactly common finds. I've learned the "bowls" were put to another use.

They were frosted, drilled through the center and turned upside down for use as a lamp shade! Collectors needing bowls are probably going to think that a waste. I hope you have your green sugar and creamer as they are getting harder than hen's teeth to locate. I have only seen the green grill plate with the pattern around the rim. Pink grill plates are found with the pattern all over and with the pattern just around the rim. Scratches show worse on the latter type.

This year you can see a yellow luncheon plate to go with the yellow cereal bowl from last year's cover.

The only newly discovered piece in Dogwood is that 6 inch plate in cremax. The darkened appearance of the piece shown isn't permanent. It's a mixture of ingenuity and oil from some equipment blended for the purpose of making the dogwood design visible to the camera and you.

Crystal Dogwood pieces are showing up, but the demand for them is very low; therefore, prices remain about the same as for those of pink even though crystal is a great deal more scarce than the pink.

One last thought. The "find" of the year turned out to be a fluke. A dealer found a yellow pitcher with blossoms similar to Dogwood. On getting it home and washing it, the "flowers" darkened and half came off. You might keep this lesson in mind when shopping. The silk screen process leaves a smooth to touch design. This faked design was coarse and gritty to the touch. Be a little skeptical of the too phenomenal find.

	PINK	GREEN	MONAX/ CREMAX
*Bowl, 5½" Cereal	3.50	4.50	10.00
Bowl, 8½" Berry	8.00	35.00	35.00
Bowl, 10¼" Fruit	60.00	55.00	
Cake Plate, 11" Heavy Solid Foot	35.00		
Cake Plate, 13" Heavy Solid Foot	30.00	27.50	
Creamer, 2½" Thin; 3¼" Thick	4.00	20.00 (Thin Only)	
Cup, Thin or Thick	2.25	3.00	25.00
Pitcher, 8", 80 oz. Decorated	55.00	285.00	
Pitcher, 8", 80 oz. (American Sweetheart Style)	350.00		
Plate, 6" Bread and Butter	1.75	2.25	20.00
*Plate, 8" Luncheon	1.50	2.00	
Plate, 9¼" Dinner	5.50		
Plate, 10½" Grill AOP or Border Design Only	4.50	7.50	
Plate, 12" Salver	6.00		30.00
Platter, 12" Oval (Rare)	90.00	125.00	
Saucer	1.50	2.00	12.50
Sherbet, Low Footed	4.50	10.00	
Sugar, 2½" Thin; 3¼" Thick	3.00	20.00 (Thin Only)	
Tid-Bit Set, 8" and 12" Plates, Center Handle	35.00	**	
Tid-Bit Set, 8", 9¼" and 12" Plates, Center Handle	55.00	**	
Tumbler, 3½", 5 oz. Decorated	50.00	**	
Tumbler, 4" 10 oz. Decorated	10.00	17.50	
Tumbler, 4¾", 11 oz. Decorated	12.00	22.50	
Tumbler, 5", 12 oz. Decorated	14.00	25.00	

*Yellow — $30.00
**Item should exist as listed in old catalogs or other publications but can not be confirmed by author.

55

DORIC

(pink, green crystal, delphite, yellow)

JEANETTE GLASS COMPANY
1935-1938

The newest addition to the Doric line is the footed green pitcher. It stands 7½ inches tall and holds 48 ounces as do the pink and yellow previously reported. That green 9 ounce tumbler has finally shown itself but not in abundance; the 5 inch cream soup mentioned in the 2nd Edition remains elusive.

Only a couple of the delphite flat bottomed Doric pitchers have come into view and very few berry sets in delphite color are in evidence. There is quite a bit of opalescent "fire" to be seen in the delphite pieces where they thin out around the design.

You will hardly find Doric sherbets in any color except delphite. They seem rather plentiful in delphite, oddly enough. I expect you will take numerous fruitless trips in search of round salad and grill plates; also,

when you search the ads for months without ever seeing the coasters at any price, you'll begin to get an idea of their present supply.

Let me clue you newcomers to the fact that the sugar and candy tops in Doric are **not** interchangeable as are those of Adam and Floral. Granted, they fit each piece and I have seen them advertised that way more than once. However, you can see by the picture that the Doric candy top is much taller and more pointed than is the sugar lid.

The cake plate for Doric is footed. The confusion over what is and what is not a cake plate in some patterns is due mostly to some companies making a heavy, flat plate and referring to it as a cake plate in their advertisements.

	PINK	GREEN	DELPHITE
Bowl, 4½" Berry	2.00	3.00	20.00
Bowl, 5" Cream Soup		35.00	
Bowl, 5½" Cereal	3.25	4.00	
Bowl, 8¼" Large Berry	6.00	7.50	60.00
Bowl, 9" Two Handled	4.50	5.00	
Bowl, 9" Oval Vegetable	5.50	6.00	
Butter Dish and Cover	35.00	40.00	
Cake Plate, 10", Three Legs	5.00	5.25	
Candy Dish and Cover, 8"	12.50	15.00	
*Candy Dish, Three Part	1.50	1.50	4.00
Coaster, 3"	5.00	5.25	
Creamer, 4"	3.00	3.25	
Cup	2.50	3.00	
Pitcher, 6", 36 oz. Flat	12.00	15.00	125.00
Pitcher, 7½", 48 oz. Footed (Also in Yellow at $300.00)	185.00	225.00	
Plate, 6" Sherbet	1.00	1.00	
Plate, 7" Salad	3.00	3.00	
Plate, 9" Dinner (Serrated 22.50)	2.50	3.00	
Plate, 9" Grill	3.00	3.00	
Platter, 12" Oval	4.50	7.50	
Relish Tray, 4" x 4"	1.50	1.75	
**Relish Tray, 4" x 8"	2.00	2.25	
Salt and Pepper, Pr.	15.00	15.00	
Saucer	1.00	1.00	
Sherbet, Footed	3.50	4.00	4.00
Sugar	3.00	3.25	
Sugar Cover	3.50	4.00	
Tray, 10" Handled	4.00	4.00	
Tray, 8" x 8" Serving	3.50	3.50	
Tumbler, 4½", 9 oz.	12.50	20.00	
Tumbler, 4", 11 oz. Flat	8.00	10.00	
Tumbler, 5", 12 oz.	8.50	10.00	

*Candy in metal holder — $35.00
**Trays in metal holder as shown — $25.00

Please refer to Foreword for pricing information

57

DORIC and PANSY

(pink, crystal, green, ultramarine)

JEANETTE GLASS COMPANY
1937-1938

The five, rarely seen Doric and Pansy pieces in the rear center of the photograph make quite a display, don't they? The butter dish was nearly impossible to find a year ago; suddenly several popped up all at once. Seeing six within three weeks time (as I did) was almost unreal! All but one of those butter dishes, I understand, have found new owners without difficulty. The Doric and Pansy shakers are difficult to get in pairs, with sharply defined patterns. Many of the shakers have very faint pansies in the panels around the top; in fact, one shaker was so bad that if it hadn't been for the color, it could hardly have passed for Doric and Pansy! The creamer and sugar are somewhat more plentiful than the butter and shakers; but there are still fewer of them to go around than there are collectors for them.

The piece of Doric and Pansy presently making the biggest advance in price is the salad plate. Salad plates have tripled in value and still the demand seems to exceed the supply.

To date, I have owned only one of the large berry bowls without handles. Hopefully, you'll be luckier than I at finding another. No new report of an ultramarine child's mug has reached my ears; but since at least one exists, there must be others.

The child's set and the berry set in pink Doric and Pansy appear to be all that exist in that color; so just quit looking for salt and pepper shakers in pink. I've an outside hope that if I use reverse psychology and say they don't exist, they'll show up. Well, it works with my sons — occasionally!

You should be aware of the varying shades of the ultramarine color. Some pieces are closer to green than the teal or ultramarine they propose to be. If you are lucky enough to find a whole set in one place, you'll probably get pieces of the same hue. Otherwise, you are going to have to put up with the color variations like the rest of us. This slight problem is graphically illustrated by the two shades of 6 inch and 9 inch plates which you see pictured.

	GREEN, TEAL	PINK, CRYSTAL		GREEN, TEAL	PINK, CRYSTAL
Bowl, 4½" Berry	4.50	3.00	Plate, 7" Salad	15.00	
Bowl, 8" Large Berry	22.50	7.00	Plate, 9" Dinner	8.50	4.50
Bowl, 9" Handled	13.00	7.50	Salt and Pepper, Pr.	325.00	
Butter Dish and Cover	600.00		Saucer	3.00	2.00
Cup	6.00	4.00	Sugar, Open	100.00	50.00
Creamer	100.00	50.00	Tray, 10" Handled	12.00	
Plate, 6" Sherbet	7.00	5.00	Tumbler, 4½", 9 oz.	20.00	

DORIC AND PANSY
"PRETTY POLLY PARTY DISHES"

	TEAL	PINK		TEAL	PINK
Cup	16.50	12.50	Creamer	25.00	15.00
Saucer	4.00	3.00	Sugar	25.00	15.00
Plate	7.00	5.00	14 Piece Set	160.00	115.00

ENGLISH HOBNAIL

(crystal, pink, amber, turquoise, cobalt, green)

WESTMORELAND GLASS COMPANY
1920's-1970's

I couldn't find enough new items to significantly improve this picture of English Hobnail; so it will have to suffice a second time. If you refer to the page of rare glass in the back of the book, however, you will see yet another color not shown here. Unfortunately, **after** we photographed, I found a creamer. and sugar to match this teal colored sherbet; it would have been nice to have shown you them, also.

Except in pink or crystal, you will have trouble completing a set of English Hobnail because its hard to find in other colors and even more difficult to match shades. There are at least three green, two yellows, two pinks, two distinct shades of turquoise, plus cobalt blue and teal blue. There's also crystal with black trim and crystal with fired on colors such as those shown by the green cologne bottle with the lilac stopper. This doesn't even take into consideration that the pieces come in both rounded and squared shapes!

For Depression lovers who have trouble distinguishing between English Hobnail and Miss America patterns, I offer the following clues. English Hobnail has a center motif with uneven rays. The Miss America motif has rays that are all equal distance from the center point. Further, the English Hobnail points curve slightly upward and are blunt on the end; the Miss America points are flat and sharp. Unfortunately, for the tumblers, this guide won't hold. English Hobnail tumblers are both round and square footed. However, with these, there are other distinguishing characteristics. The English Hobnail goblets flair out slightly at the rim and the pattern stops toward the rims on a plain field of glass. The Miss America goblets don't flair out and they all have a set of rings above the pattern hobs before it goes to plain glass toward the rim.

	COBALT, AMBER, TURQUOISE* PINK, GREEN
**Ash Tray, Several Shapes	10.00
Bowls, 4½", 5" Square and Round	7.00
Bowl, Cream Soup	7.00
Bowls, 6", Several Styles	8.00
Bowls, 8", Several Styles	12.50
**Bowls, 8" Footed and Two Handled	27.50
**Bowls, 11" and 12" Nappies	27.50
Bowls, Relish, Oval, 8", 9"	12.50
Bowl, Relish, Oval, 12"	13.00
Candlesticks, 3½", Pair	20.00
Candlesticks, 8½", Pair	27.50
Candy Dish, ½ Lb., Cone Shaped	27.50
Candy Dish and Cover, Three Feet	22.50
Celery Dish, 9"	10.00
Celery Dish, 12"	15.00
**Cigarette Box	15.00
**Cologne Bottle	19.00
Creamer, Footed or Flat	7.00
Cup	5.00
Decanter, 20 oz. with Stopper	30.00
Demitasse Cup and Saucer	15.00
Egg Cup	20.00
Goblet, 1 oz. Cordial	7.50
Goblet, 2 oz. Wine	8.00
Goblet, 3 oz. Cocktail	8.00

*Add about 50% more for Turquoise
**Cobalt double price listed

	COBALT, AMBER, TURQUOISE* PINK, GREEN
Goblet, 5 oz. Claret	10.00
**Goblet, 6¼", 8 oz.	12.50
Grapefruit, 6½", Flange Rim	7.00
Lamp, 6¼", Electric	40.00
**Lamp, 9¼"	45.00
Lampshade, 17" Diameter	85.00
Marmalade and Cover	20.00
Pitcher, 23 oz.	35.00
Pitcher, 39 oz.	37.50
Pitcher, 60 oz.	50.00
Pitcher, ½ Gal. Straight Sides	35.00
**Plate, 5½", 6½", Sherbet	2.25
Plate, 7¼", Pie	3.00
**Plate, 8" Round or Square	5.00
Plate, 10" Dinner	7.00
Salt and Pepper, Pr., Round or Square Bases	20.00
Salt Dip, 2", Footed and with Place Card Holder	5.00
Saucer	2.00
**Sherbet	7.50
Sugar, Footed or Flat	7.00
Tumbler, 3¾", 5 oz. or 8 oz.	6.00
Tumbler, 4", 10 oz. Iced Tea	7.50
Tumbler, 5", 12 oz. Iced Tea	7.50
Tumbler, 7 oz., Footed	8.00
Tumbler, 9 oz., Footed	9.00
Tumbler, 12½ oz., Footed	9.00
Whiskey, 1½ oz. and 3 oz.	6.50

Please refer to Foreword for pricing information

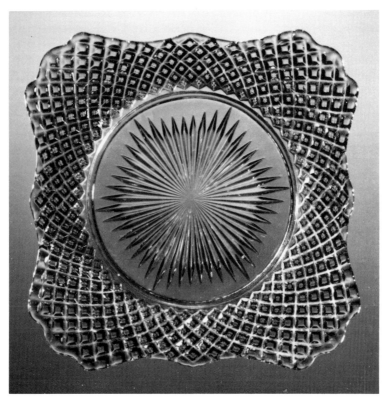

61

FLORAGOLD, "LOUISA"

(iridescent, pink, blue, green)

JEANETTE GLASS COMPANY
1950's

I imagine the rose bowl on the cover caught your eye. It did mine, too, when I bought it just before we photographed; so I gambled and put it in the cover shot. Now that I've done my homework, I find that this is a piece of "Louisa" carnival glass, the glass Floragold was patterned after. Yes, I do those things, too; only when I mess up, I do it big! Anyway, now that it's there, let's make use of it to learn something. That's a standard carnival piece even though the pattern fits Floragold to a "T"; and why shouldn't it! I still think it's a clever little piece; but I apologize for my blissful ignorance at the time we photographed. What a find it almost was!

Several items in Floragold have made hops, skips and even jumps in price. In that last category you may fit the candy dish, shakers and the tray with indent. In fact, I've separated the two trays this time because the plain tray is readily available; but the indented tray is nearly as impossible as finding a goose laying golden eggs.

A celery or vase, made from the same mold as a large tumbler but which is crumpled at the top, made its debut recently. Ash trays, plates, sherbets and the round butter dish in Floragold still appear infrequently. The price listed for shakers is with perfect white or brown tops. Shakers with cracked tops (caused from screwing them down too tightly) bring about half the price of mint condition shakers. In other words, the top of Floragold shakers is the hard part to find and not the shakers themselves.

Quite a few boxes of egg nog sets are turning up. Some contain a large bowl and cups while others have the pitcher and cups. So far, while the boxed sets are nice to have the boxes are of little value except to confirm the way the pieces were originally sold. Remember, this glass was issued in the 1950's and strictly speaking, though collected by Depression Glass devotees, this is not Depression Glass.

The shell pink color shown was made in the late fifties and is shown here simply for the novelty item it is. You will also find tall open candies or fruit stands in ice blue, crystal or a red-yellow combination. These items were made as late as 1969 and 1970.

	IRIDESCENT
Bowl, 4½" Square	1.50
Bowl, 5½" Cereal Round	4.50
Bowl, 5½" Ruffled Fruit	1.75
Bowl, 8½" Ruffled Fruit	1.00
Bowl, 9½" Salad, Deep	10.00
Bowl, 12" Ruffled, Large Fruit	4.00
Butter Dish and Cover	
¼ lb. Oblong	8.00
Butter Dish and Cover, Round	27.50
Candlesticks, Double	
Branch, Pr.	12.00
Candy or Cheese Dish	
and Cover, 6¾"	16.00
Candy, 5¼" Long, 5 Feet	2.00
Coaster — Ash Tray, 4"	3.25

	IRIDESCENT
Creamer	2.50
Cup	3.00
Pitcher, 64 oz.	12.00
Plate, 5¾" Sherbet	1.25
Plate, 8½" Dinner	7.50
Plate or Tray, 13½"	7.00
Indent on 13½" Plate	22.00
Platter, 11¼"	10.00
Salt and Pepper, Plastic Tops	22.00
Saucer	2.50
Sherbet, Low Footed	3.00
Sugar	2.50
Sugar Lid	2.00
Tumbler, 10 oz., Footed	7.25
Tumbler, 11 oz., Footed	9.00
Tumbler, 15 oz., Footed	12.50

FLORAL "POINSETTA"

(pink, green, delphite, jadite, crystal, amber)   **JEANETTE GLASS COMPANY 1931-1935**

A collector of Floral in Atlanta said she just couldn't wait to open this book and see what was new. Well, I can't offer the **number** of new pieces the last book included; but there are a few goodies to report! For instance, pictured on the page with rare glass at the back of the book is the delphite Floral platter and the 9 inch comport (an old word for compote which is used in the company catalogue listings of the time, fledgelings). I hope the panelled juice, the delphite tumbler and the pink and green Floral ice tubs on the cover weren't overlooked; and a large pink ruffled berry bowl to match the small one pictured before has turned up, as well as a green Floral oval vegetable WITH COVER. Are those sufficiently interesting for the time being?

Those Floral ice tubs have really jumped in price as they seem quite rare and many collectors are still looking for them to add to their collections. Grill plates in green Floral are few and far between which is a fate only slightly better than the none-at-all one being suffered in pink. The flared out three legged vase shown in green and the crystal bowl are one-of-a-kind to date. A small oval tray of undetermined use measuring 9¼ inch by 6 inches was found at the Atlanta show last year. It came from Texas but I didn't trace its history further than that.

All of the really unusual pieces, except for the comport, have turned up in green. We can hope that some will turn up in pink to sort of equalize the frustration levels now being enjoyed only by the collectors of green Floral.

Sorry, but I haven't been able to round up anothr pair of tall green Floral shakers since I sold those for $6.00 way back when. I did see a pair advertised lately at about "pink" price. Lucky somebody, eh? At that, I'll bet they made more than I did on the ones I sold!

The delphite Floral items are of such limited quantity that they have little chance to gain in popularity; they are extremely rare, however; so don't let them slip by you if you get lucky enough to find some.

Remember to look for the lamp made from a sherbet that was frosted inside, notched to accommodate a switch, and covered with a metal top into which a chimney bulb fitted. One is pictured at top left. The sherbet-like base is rather frequently found; unfortunately, it's the metal part and the chimney style bulb which make the piece a "find".

	PINK	GREEN	DELPHITE	JADITE
Bowl, 4" Berry (Ruffled 17.50)	1.50	1.50	20.00	
Bowl, 5½" Cream Soup		35.00		
Bowl, 7½" Salad (Ruffled 30.00)	4.00	4.00	40.00	
Bowl, 8" Covered Vegetable	12.50	15.00	35.00 (no cover)	
*Bowl, 9" Oval Vegetable	4.25	6.00		
Butter Dish and Cover	42.50	47.50		
Canister Set: Coffee, Tea, Cereal, Sugar, 5¼" Tall Set				40.00
Candlesticks, 4" Pr.	17.50	25.00		
Candy Jar and Cover	12.50	17.50		
Creamer, Flat	3.50	3.50	40.00	
Coaster, 3¼"	4.00	4.50		
Comport, 9"	150.00	150.00		
†Cup	3.00	3.25		
Ice Tub, Oval, 3½" High	175.00	175.00		
Lamp	60.00	60.00		
Pitcher, 5½", 23 or 24 oz.		350.00		
Pitcher, 8", 32 oz. Footed Cone	9.00	12.50		
Pitcher, 10¼", 48 oz. Lemonade	90.00	110.00		
Plate, 6" Sherbet	1.25	1.25		
Plate, 8" Salad	2.00	2.00		
†Plate, 9" Dinner	3.00	3.00	40.00	
Plate, 9" Grill		17.50		
Platter, 10¾" Oval	4.00	4.25	50.00	
Refrigerator Dish and Cover, 5" Square	12.50	17.50		10.00
††Relish Dish, Oval, Two Part	2.50	2.50		
Salt and Pepper, Pr., 4" Footed	15.00	22.50		
Salt and Pepper, 6" Flat	15.00	100.00		
†Saucer	1.25	1.25		
Sherbet	3.50	4.00	50.00	
Sugar	3.50	3.50	40.00 (open)	
Sugar/Candy Cover	3.50	4.00		
Tray, 6" Square, Closed Handles	4.00	4.00		
Tray, 9¼"		150.00		
Tumbler, 4", 5 oz. Footed Juice	5.50	6.50		
Tumbler, 4¾", 7 oz. Footed Water	6.00	7.00	75.00	
Tumbler, 5¼", 9 oz. Footed Lemonade	12.00	12.00		
Vase, 3 Legged Rose Bowl		250.00		
Vase, 3 Legged Flared (Also in Crystal)		250.00		
Vase, 6¼" Tall (8 Sided)		250.00		

†These have now been found in amber.
††This has been found in yellow.
*Covered in Green — 37.50

Please refer to Foreword for pricing information

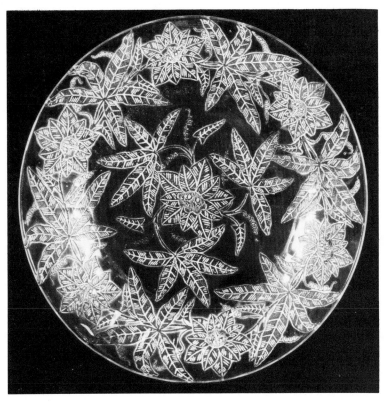

FLORAL AND DIAMOND BAND

(crystal, pink, green)

JENKINS GLASS COMPANY
1927-1931

It is my understanding that beautiful diamonds are first found in the rough. Yet this heavy Floral and Diamond Band pattern with its badly molded pieces has not enticed many collectors; thus I assume this expectant attitude doesn't hold true in glass collection.

Believe it or not, once Floral and Diamond Band is on the table, it makes an attractive setting. If you're a coffee addict, it has the drawback of having no cup and saucer, however.

The pattern is reminiscent of older glass. I think this is especially borne out by the fact that you find a few pieces with etched flowers on both sides. Look closely at the small, green sugar shown. I've recently

found a sugar and creamer set with this pattern, but etched in a similar manner. These are further oddities when you consider that most Depression Glass etching was done on otherwise plain glassware. Most of this mass produced glass was aimed at quantity production rather than quality; so why take the time to etch flowers into an already patterned glass?

A few pieces of iridescent Floral and Diamond Band have been noted; in fact, I added one to a collector's pitcher collection. I regret it didn't make it back to me in time to be photographed as we'd planned.

I tried to change the pink sugar to green or the green lid to pink for the picture, but the genie wasn't a bit cooperative.

	GREEN/PINK
Bowl, 4½" Berry	2.50
Bowl, 5¾" Nappy, Handled	3.00
Bowl, 8" Large Berry	5.50
Butter Dish and Cover	50.00
Compote, 5½" Tall	5.00
Creamer, Small	3.00
Creamer, 4¾"	7.00

*Iridescent — $75.00

*Iridescent slightly higher and sometimes called "Mayflower" by Carnival glass collectors.

	GREEN/PINK
*Pitcher, 8", 42 oz.	40.00
Plate, 8" Luncheon	3.00
Sherbet	2.75
Sugar, Small	3.00
Sugar, 5¼"	7.00
Sugar Lid	10.00
Tumbler, 4" Water	5.75
Tumbler, 5" Iced Tea	10.00

FLORENTINE NO. 1, "POPPY NO. 1"

(pink, green, crystal, yellow, cobalt) **HAZEL ATLAS GLASS COMPANY 1932-1935**

Since we are using the same Florentine No. 1 picture here that we did in the second edition, I will have to restate that the eight pieces down the left hand side of the photograph are all Florentine No. 2 and will be described under that pattern. For those of you who have not seen the previous books, we used some of the color shots from the first book in the second; and the Florentine No. 2 shot was one of those. Thus, in order to show the unusual pieces that had surfaced in Florentine No. 2 between book one and two, I elected to include them in this picture rather than to not have them included at all. I hope all that is not too confusing.

You can see an unusual Florentine ice tea pictured at the right rear. This tumbler is from the Floral iced tea mold but has the Florentine pattern on it. This would not be too unusual a circumstance if these two patterns had been made by the same company; but they were not, and therein lies the mystery. One possible solution was offered by the daughter of a glass worker at Hazel Atlas. He recalls that many of the companies used to exchange glass molds. This is another reason those of us who try to research older glass company products get headaches though I assure you that this is only one of many reasons!

Collectors have found out that the ruffled creamers and sugars in Florentine No. 1 are much harder to find than the covered versions, particularly in the green or yellow colors. The smaller coaster/ash trays are in hiding more than their bigger brothers, also.

Butter dishes in all colors have made advances in price as have shakers.

Demand for crystal Florentine No. 1 still continues to wane except for the elusive butter dish which brings as much as does the green. Other than that, you can price the remaining crystal pieces at twenty to twenty-five per cent lower than the green.

	GREEN	YELLOW	PINK	BLUE
Ash Tray, 5½"	10.00	15.00	17.50	
Bowl, 5" Berry	1.25	3.00	4.00	9.50
Bowl, 6" Cereal	3.00	4.00	4.50	
Bowl, 8½" Large Berry	6.00	10.00	11.50	
Bowl, 9½" Oval Vegetable	6.00	9.00	10.00	
Butter Dish and Cover	65.00	90.00	135.00	
Coaster/Ash Tray, 3¾"	7.50	7.50	15.00	
Creamer	2.50	3.00	5.00	
Creamer, Ruffled	10.00	10.00	10.00	35.00
Cup	1.75	2.00	3.00	
Pitcher, 6½", 36 oz. Footed	17.50	25.00	27.50	
Pitcher, 7½", 54 oz. Flat, Ice Lip or None	27.50	75.00	75.00	
Plate, 6" Sherbet	1.00	1.00	1.25	
Plate, 8½" Salad	1.50	1.50	2.00	
Plate, 10" Dinner	3.00	3.50	4.00	
Plate, 10" Grill	2.00	2.50	2.50	
Platter, 11½" Oval	4.00	4.00	5.00	
Salt and Pepper, Footed	15.00	22.50	30.00	
Saucer	1.00	1.00	1.25	
Sherbet, 3 oz. Footed	3.00	4.00	4.50	
Sugar	2.50	3.00	5.00	
Sugar Cover	5.00	7.00	7.00	
Sugar, Ruffled	10.00	10.00	10.00	35.00
Tumbler, 3¾", 5 oz. Footed Juice	4.50	7.00	9.00	
Tumbler, 4¾", 10 oz. Footed Water	7.50	8.00	10.00	
Tumbler, 5¼", 12 oz. Footed Iced Tea	8.50	9.00	12.50	
Tumbler, 5¼", 9 oz. Lemonade (Like Floral)			35.00	

Please refer to Foreword for pricing information

FLORENTINE NO. 2, "POPPY NO. 2"

(pink, green, yellow, crystal, cobalt blue) **HAZEL ATLAS GLASS COMPANY 1934-1937**

First of all, the eight pieces shown on the left hand side of the Florentine No. 1 picture (see first paragraph explanation) need to be taken care of! The large pink and small berry bowls are not exactly your common everyday pieces, nor are the cobalt blue items. That shaker is a fired on blue and not a pure cobalt as are the other pieces. Those blown tumblers are 3½ inches tall and hold 6 ounces.

The amber footed tumbler shown here and on the cover is 4 inches tall and has a 5 ounce capacity. This must have been an experimental batch of glass as some other pieces (previously listed here) have shown up.

That green pitcher in the rear of the picture and the yellow pitcher without the ice lip which was pictured in the first two books are being listed under both Florentine No. 1 and No. 2. To justify this, I offer the following ideas. The pitcher has been found in an original box with the Florentine No. 2 tumblers which seem to indicate it belongs with Florentine No. 2; however, a letter from a reader of the second book points out that the handle shape of this pitcher is similar to the shape of the footed Florentine No. 1 pitcher and not like the one of Florentine No. 2. In this case I would go along with that logic had the pitcher not been found with those No. 2 tumblers. So, for now, the pitcher is listed both places; you may take your pick as to where it really belongs.

Let's try to eliminate a few of the problems about the two sizes of footed, cone shaped pitchers in Florentine No. 2. The common 7⅛ inch tall (to the lip) pitcher holds 28 ounces to the brim and on some will go as high as 29½ ounces before spilling out the lip. The shorter, chubbier 6¼ inch pitcher holds 24 to 25½ ounces before the "ooops". There's a lot of variation in measuring the capacity of a pitcher; and I've added as much as an extra eight ounces above what an old catalogue listing says the pitcher will hold. I personally feel its capacity should be whatever amount of liquid it will hold before it spills out the lip.

Demand for crystal Florentine No. 2 remains strong and that is why it is priced with the green here. In fact, the crystal butter dish may be the toughest of all the butters to find. Candy dishes have never been common in any color; yet those you do find may be damaged due to use; so pay particular attention to the inside rims.

That crystal plate in front has an indent fitting the custard cup or jello. The cup strayed on its way to be photographed and that is why you don't see it.

Notice in the listing the many pieces in pink that have never yet shown up; keep them in the back of your mind in case you're lucky enough to see them.

	CRYSTAL, GREEN	PINK	YELLOW	BLUE
Ash Tray, 2½"			15.00	
Bowl, 4½" Berry	2.00	4.50	3.00	
Bowl, 4¾" Cream Soup	3.00	4.50	6.50	
Bowl, 5" Cream Soup, or Ruffled Nut		4.00		25.00
Bowl, 6" Cereal	3.00	7.00	6.50	
Bowl, 8" Large Berry	6.00	12.00	7.50	
Bowl, 9" Oval Vegetable and Cover	9.00		14.00	
*Butter Dish and Cover	50.00		60.00	
Candlesticks, 2¾", Pr.	17.50		22.50	
Candy Dish and Cover	45.00	70.00	60.00	
Coaster, 3¼"	7.00	9.00	9.00	
Coaster/Ash Tray, 3¾"	7.00		9.00	
Coaster/Ash Tray, 5½"	9.00		12.00	
Comport, 3½" Ruffled	7.50	4.50	10.00	40.00
Creamer	3.00		3.50	
Cup (Amber: 30.00)	2.50		3.00	
Custard Cup or Jello	7.00		10.00	
Gravy Boat			15.00	
Pitcher, 6¼", 24 oz. Cone Footed			65.00	
†Pitcher, 7½", 28 oz. Cone Footed	11.00		10.00	
Pitcher, 7½", 54 oz.	27.50	75.00	75.00	
Pitcher, 8", 76 oz.	30.00		95.00	
Plate, 6" Sherbet	1.00		1.50	

* Crystal— $90.00

	CRYSTAL, GREEN	PINK	YELLOW	BLUE
Plate, 6¼" with Indent	5.00		6.00	
Plate, 8½" Salad	1.50	2.25	2.25	
Plate, 10" Dinner	3.00	4.00	4.00	
Plate, 10¼" Grill	2.50		2.50	
Platter, 11" Oval	4.00	6.00	6.00	
Platter, 11½" for Gravyboat			17.50	
Relish Dish, 10", 3 Part or Plain	4.00	6.00	7.50	
††Salt and Pepper, Pr.	17.50		27.50	
Saucer (Amber: 12.50)	1.25		1.50	
Sherbet, Footed (Amber: 30.00)	3.00		4.50	
Sugar	3.00		3.50	
Sugar Cover	3.00		4.00	
Tray, Condiment for Shakers Creamer and Sugar (Round)			25.00	
Tumbler, 3½", 5 oz. Juice	4.00	5.00	5.50	
Tumbler, 3½", 6 oz. Blown	7.00			
†††Tumbler, 4" 9 oz. Water	5.00	5.00	6.00	40.00
Tumbler, 5" 12 oz. Iced Tea	8.50		12.00	
Tumbler, 3¼", 5 oz. Footed	5.00		6.50	
Tumbler, 4", 5 oz. Footed	5.00		7.50	
Tumbler, 4½", 9 oz. Footed	8.00		8.00	
Tumbler, 5", 12 oz. Footed	9.00		12.00	
Vase or Parfait, 6"	10.00		17.50	

†Blue — $300.00
††Fired-on Orange or Blue, Pr. — 20.00
†††Amber: — 40.00

71

FLOWER GARDEN WITH BUTTERFLIES, "BUT-TERFLIES AND ROSES"

(pink, green, blue-green, canary yellow, amber)

U. S. GLASS COMPANY
Late 1920's

I'm betting that this picture of Flower Garden with Butterflies in color is going to send more collectors for their butterfly nets! My wife thinks this pattern pretty and frankly, she's a little hard to excite about some of this glass. I warn you of two things in advance: 1) there isn't much of it to go around, and 2) even knowing that there's a butterfly somewhere in that jumble of roses, it's going to be a trick to find it.

The sandwich server in Flower Garden with Butterflies is the newest item shown though several more unusual items have been found since the photograph was taken. From Pennsylvania has come a report of a pair of black amethyst wall sconces; and a rolled edge console bowl has turned up to match the little 7 inch black vase pictured.

That poor pink saucer has been without a cup for a couple of years. Surely someone out there can discover one!

Notice the two styles of 8 inch plates. The pink has a narrow band around its edge while the green has no rim whatsoever.

The amber plate in the right rear has an indent for a compote and it is listed as a cheese and cracker set. Wouldn't one in the canary yellow or blue be pretty? I did see a satin or frosted piece, but it wasn't exactly the most exciting piece I've ever seen.

I've seen a canary yellow vase in Flower Garden with Butterflies and you may believe me when I say that the canary yellow is as pretty as the blue — and I'm by nature partial to the color blue.

All in all, the little ash tray and holder is the item I'm most charmed by in this pattern. I could hardly believe what I was seeing when I found that!

	ALL COLORS*
Ash Tray, Match-Pack Holders	10.00
Bowl, Rolled Edge Console	25.00
Candlesticks, 4", Pr.	13.50
Candlesticks, 8", Pr.	17.50
Candy Dish and Cover, 8"	15.00
Candy Dish, Open, 6"	7.50
Cheese and Cracker Set	
(4" Compote, 10" Plate)	20.00
Cologne Bottle, 7½", Tall Footed	10.00
Console Bowl, 10" Footed	20.00
Creamer	9.50

	ALL COLORS*
Cup	7.50
Plate, 8", Two Styles	6.00
Powder Jar, Footed	12.50
Powder Jar, Flat	8.00
Sandwich Server, center handle	20.00
Saucer	4.00
Sugar, Open	9.50
Tray, 5½" x 10" Oval	12.50
Tray, Rectangular, 11¾" x 7¾"	15.00
Vase, 7" (Black)	45.00
Vase, 10"	27.50

Design on Black highlighted to emphasize pattern.

*Add 25% for blue or black items.

Please refer to Foreword for pricing information

73

"FORTUNE"

(pink, crystal)

HOCKING GLASS COMPANY
1937-1938

The name for "Fortune" came from "some-one" and not from the company itself. As you can see, this is not a very large pattern nor is it the most cherished by collectors.

The most desirable piece for candy dish collectors is the candy bowl in pink.

There is a strong possibility that the pitcher does exist although I haven't found any material from Hocking to indicate this. I have, however, received snapshots from two collectors who have pitchers that look very similar to the Fortune pattern.

It's possible you might find your own small fortune by turning up a pink Fortune pitcher with six tumblers in the original box! Keep looking.

	PINK, CRYSTAL
Bowl, 4" Berry	.75
Bowl, 4½" Dessert	.75
Bowl, 4½" Handled	.75
Bowl, 5¼" Rolled Edge	1.25
Bowl, 7¾" Salad or Large Berry	2.00
Candy Dish and Cover, Flat	6.00

	PINK, CRYSTAL
Cup	1.50
Plate, 6" Sherbet	1.00
Plate, 8" Luncheon	1.50
Saucer	.75
Tumbler, 3½", 5 oz. Juice	1.25
Tumbler, 4", 9 oz. Water	1.75

75

"FRUITS"

(pink, green, crystal)

HAZEL ATLAS AND OTHER GLASS COMPANIES
1931-1933

The best think I could say about "Fruits" is that there are plenty of different tumblers to collect if you are a tumbler collector. In following last book's lead of adding several companies here, we can add a 3½" juice tumbler with cherries only on it. As the phrase goes, "at this point in time" I have not seen a pink pitcher with cherries motif (like the one pictured here in green), but they surely must exist judging by the number of pink tumblers around.

Reported to me, but unconfirmed, was a Fruits platter out of eastern Kentucky.

I keep running into iridescent "Pears" tumblers priced very high although they are rather commonly found; and no matter what you are told, these are not carnival glass.

The tumbler with Cherries only which matches the pitcher is the one most in demand by collectors — especially in green.

Crystal pieces bring as little as fifty per cent of the prices for pink and green simply due to the lack of collectors for the crystal.

	PINK, GREEN
Bowl, 5" Cereal	2.00
Bowl, 8" Berry	9.00
Cup	2.00
Pitcher, 7" Flat Bottom	27.50

	PINK, GREEN
Plate, 8" Luncheon	2.50
Saucer	1.00
Sherbet	2.25
Tumbler, 3½", Juice	3.00
Tumbler, 4" (One Fruit)	6.00
Tumbler, 4" (Combination of Fruits)	5.50

GEORGIAN, "LOVEBIRDS"

(green, crystal)

FEDERAL GLASS COMPANY
1931-1936

New collectors of Depression Glass will note that the "lovebirds" alternate in the design with a basket of flowers.

Collectors have searched high and low for the Georgian bowl pictured in the very front. It is the most difficult item to locate in this pattern although the tall iced tea tumbler runs it a close second.

The sugar lids for both of the sugars are interchangeable, but they are not easily found in mint condition. I trust by now you have noted that all sugar lids are priced separately in this book. I started to do this last time and now wish I had in order to keep some people from buying common sugar bowls at high prices when it is the lid that is hard to find and not the sugar bowl itself.

The challenge for a Georgian cream soup went unanswered; so we'll have to conclude it doesn't exist.

For collectors who are confused about the differences in plates, the plate on the left has the center design and pattern around the rim only while the one on the right is the regular type plate.

Georgian hot plates are similar to the center design plates and the sugar lids. There are no tell-tale "lovebirds" on them; so you need to be familiar with the center design also.

A few more walnut lazy susans with Georgian hot plates have surfaced; so be on the lookout for them. Refer to the Madrid pattern to see what one should look like.

One item that people seem to overlook is the Georgian platter. It's been quite a while since I have even seen one; so remember I told you so!

	GREEN
Bowl, 4½" Berry	1.75
Bowl, 5¾" Cereal	3.00
Bowl, 6½" Deep	15.00
Bowl, 7½" Large Berry	8.00
Bowl, 9" Oval Vegetable	7.50
Butter Dish and Cover	40.00
Cold Cuts Server, 18½" Wood with Seven 5" Openings for 5" Coasters	250.00
Creamer, 3" Footed	3.25
Creamer, 4" Footed	4.00
Cup	2.50

†Crystal: 20.00

	GREEN
†Hot Plate, 5" Center Design	16.00
Plate, 6" Sherbet	1.00
Plate, 8" Luncheon	2.00
Plate, 9¼" Dinner	3.00
Plate, 9¼" Center Design Only	2.75
Platter, 11½" Closed Handled	7.50
Saucer	1.25
Sherbet	4.00
Sugar, 3" Footed	3.25
Sugar, 4" Footed	4.00
Sugar Cover	3.00
Tumbler, 4", 9 oz. Flat	10.00
Tumbler, 5¼", 12 oz. Flat	15.00

Please refer to Foreword for pricing information

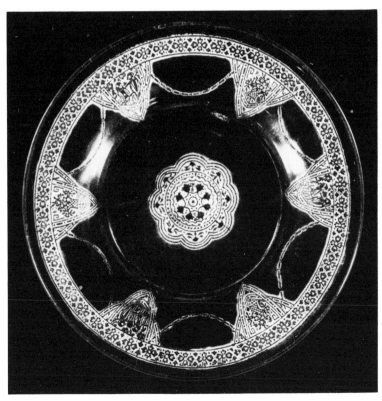

79

HERITAGE

(crystal, pink, blue, green)

FEDERAL GLASS COMPANY
Late 1930's-1960's

In the first book, I listed pink, blue and green colors for Heritage. By the time I wrote the second, I could still only confirm blue and pink colors; naturally, a week after that book went to press, I found a large green bowl and six smaller green ones in a dark, extremely dirty corner of a shop in Ohio. I ruined a perfectly clean sheet wrapping them very carefully on my way to a show. (The shop didn't believe in using paper to wrap; so my display sheet had to suffice.) The plot thickens in the search for Heritage, though; so read on.

Not long ago I made a hasty call to a dealer advertising some green Heritage only to hear, to my dismay, that a dealer in Georgia had snapped it up. I then called Georgia and was promised to be remembered should said merchandise ever be for sale. A few days later I got a call from Georgia offering the complete set very reasonably. It seemed that the green Heritage looked mighty like avocado green "Daisy" upon arrival. I had to laugh, but I was sorry to hear that only

the berry set seems to exist so far. I'm certain you've gotten the message by now that dealers would consider green Heritage quite a "find"; so scout around.

Blue Heritage is quite pretty, but terribly shy about showing itself. I was told about a blue saucer a couple of years ago, but since the snapshot I was promised never materialized and since I've not heard anything more, I'm removing it from the list. Should you find this, or any other unlisted or doubted-in-existence color, I'd really appreciate a snapshot. Your glass is sometimes the best resource material available!

Gold trimmed crystal Heritage can be found; but I warn you that sugars and creamers in crystal, gold trimmed or otherwise, are not very plentiful. Also, the 8½ inch berry bowl in crystal is more difficult to find than the 10½ inch fruit bowl.
'Fess up, now; you didn't even recognize the Heritage pieces on the cover as being Heritage.

	CRYSTAL	PINK	BLUE	GREEN
Bowl, 5″ Berry	1.50	7.00	12.00	12.00
Bowl, 8½″ Large Berry	6.00	12.00	20.00	20.00
Bowl, 10½″, Fruit	5.50			
Cup	2.00			
Creamer, Footed	4.50			
Plate, 8″ Luncheon	2.00			
Plate, 9¼″ Dinner	3.50			
Plate, 12″ Sandwich	4.00			
Saucer	1.00			
Sugar, Open, Footed	4.50			

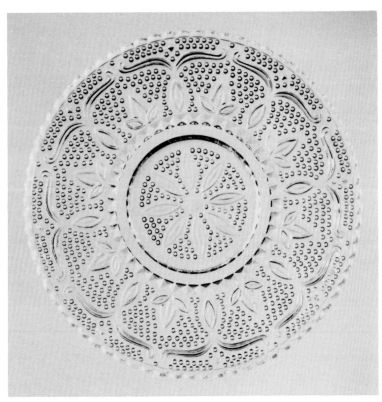

81

HEX OPTIC, "HONEYCOMB"

(pink, green)

JEANETTE GLASS COMPANY
1928-1932

Finally, the Hex Optic pitcher with the Floral lemonade pitcher shape makes it appearance!

There were many companies that made hexagonal designed glass, but Jeanette's Hex Optic is characterized by being a heavy, bulky glass.

Since many of you are using Depression Glass in your kitchen decor, you might consider the Hex Optic stacking set or ice pail (metal handle missing) in the picture. That lip on the latter could make it sub as a pitcher in a pinch.

The small Hex Optic pitcher with a sunflower design in the bottom tends to con-

fuse readers who mistake it for a Sunflower pitcher. This was made by the same company which made Sunflower but this design was used in the bottom of a number of pieces including some made in delphite and jadite.

As Hex Optic was a heavy, utilitarian line of glassware, you will find many of the pieces are badly scratched or rubbed from long periods of use. The mixing bowls found in this pattern tend to show the worst usage scars of any pieces.

You may find some iridescent tumblers shaped like the ones shown; these are of much later vintage, however, having been made in the late 50's or early 60's.

	PINK, GREEN		PINK, GREEN
Bowl, 4¼" Berry, Ruffled	1.25	Plate, 8" Luncheon	1.50
Bowl, 7½" Large Berry	3.00	Platter, 11" Round	4.00
Butter Dish and Cover, Rectangular		Refrigerator Dish	3.00
1 Pound Size	10.00	Salt and Pepper, Pr.	10.00
Creamer, 2 Style Handles	2.00	Saucer	1.00
Cup, 2 Style Handles	1.50	Sugar, 2 Styles of Handles	2.00
Ice Bucket, Metal Handle	7.00	Sherbet, 5 oz. Footed	2.00
Pitcher, 5", 32 oz. Sunflower		Tumbler, 3¾", 9 oz.	2.00
Motif in Bottom	5.00	Tumbler, 5¾", Footed	3.00
Pitcher, 9", 48 oz. Footed	17.50	Tumbler, 7" Footed	4.00
Plate, 6" Sherbet	1.00	Whiskey, 2", 1 oz.	2.50

Please refer to Foreword for pricing information

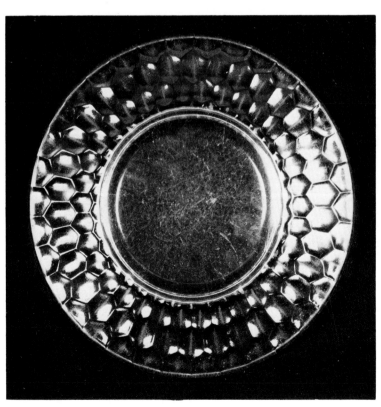

83

HOBNAIL

(crystal, pink)

HOCKING GLASS COMPANY
1934-1936

The pink pitcher and tumblers included here are "Hobnail" but were made by Macbeth Evans rather than Hocking. However, since no pink Hobnail pitcher and tumblers have shown up in Hocking's pattern, a number of people are buying the Macbeth Evans product to go with their otherwise Hocking collection. They do blend well with the pattern; so I felt that others of you might want to add to your few pink pieces by doing this also. Hence their being pictured here.

Notice the similarity in the shapes of Hobnail and those of Miss America. They were both made by Hocking.

The small milk pitcher in crystal Hobnail

has the same lines as its larger brother.

That little footed whiskey shown holds only 1½ ounces and would fit well in anyone's miniature collection.

The Hobnail pieces trimmed in red, illustrated by the plate shown here, make decorative accessory pieces particularly when presented on a dark background.

Although Hobnail thus far has only four actual pieces in pink, it does have quite a variety in crystal. However, don't let that fact mislead you into thinking it an easy pattern to assemble. Finding pieces in this takes a bit of looking; should you choose to do so, I think you'll be pleased to find it a pattern with a lot of style.

	PINK	CRYSTAL
Bowl, 5½" Cereal		.50
Bowl, 7" Salad		1.25
Cup	1.50	1.00
Creamer, Footed		1.25
Decanter and Stopper, 32 oz.		10.00
Goblet, 10 oz. Water		3.75
Goblet, 18 oz. Iced Tea		4.50
Pitcher, 18 oz. Milk		8.50
Pitcher, 67 oz.		12.00
Plate, 6" Sherbet	1.00	.50
Plate, 8½" Luncheon	1.50	1.00

	PINK	CRYSTAL
Saucer (Sherbet Plate in Pink)	1.00	.50
Sherbet	1.50	1.25
Sugar, Footed		1.25
Tumbler, 5 oz. Juice		3.00
Tumbler, 9 oz., 10 oz. Water		4.50
Tumbler, 15 oz. Iced Tea		5.00
Tumbler, 3 oz. Footed Wine		3.75
Tumbler, 5 oz. Footed Cordial		3.50
Whiskey, 1½ oz.		2.50

85

HOLIDAY, "BUTTON AND BOWS"

(pink, iridescent)

JEANETTE GLASS COMPANY
1947-1949

Holiday, as is the case with Anniversary, is not truly a Depression era glass. It was made in the late 1940's and was patterned after the older Daisy and Button dishes or "Button and Bows" as so many people commonly called it. For such a late issue, there are quite a number of items that are hard to get. You can see by the jumps in prices made by several items that they have been found to be in limited supply.

The Holiday cake plate and the tall, footed tumbler have always been bad news to find; but the item that has slipped by a lot of you is that large chop plate. Getting harder and harder are Holiday footed juices and candlesticks. If you are to have these in your set, you'd better get to buying it right away.

The 10¾ inch footed console is still around; it was issued also in the shell pink opaque

in the late 1950's. Other fifties issues were the iridized pieces, such as platters, small pitchers and footed juices.

That plentiful supply of butter dishes of a few years ago is gradually drying up.

The small Holiday milk pitcher has finally passed the larger in price due to its being a great deal more scarce and lots of collectors prefer it to go with their footed juices.

New collectors of Holiday should note that there are two sizes of cups and that cups fitting the rayed saucers are not interchangeable with the plain saucers. So check to see if your cup bottom is plain or rayed, as the saucer ring will have to match the bottom of the cup it fits.

	PINK
Bowl, 5⅛" Berry	2.25
Bowl, 7¾" Soup	9.75
Bowl, 8½" Large Berry	5.00
Bowl, 9½" Oval Vegetable	4.00
Bowl, 10¾" Console	15.00
Butter Dish and Cover	22.50
Cake Plate, 10½", 3 Legged	25.00
Candlesticks, 3", Pr.	22.50
Creamer, Footed	2.50
Cup, Two Sizes	2.25
Pitcher, 4¾", 16 oz. Milk	15.00
Pitcher, 6¾", 52 oz.	12.50

	PINK
Plate, 6" Sherbet	1.00
Plate, 9" Dinner	2.75
Plate, 13¾" Chop	27.50
Platter, 11⅜" Oval	4.00
Sandwich Tray, 10½"	5.00
Saucer, Two Styles	1.25
Sherbet	3.25
Sugar	2.50
Sugar Cover	2.00
Tumbler, 4", 10 oz. Flat	6.00
Tumbler, 4", Footed	12.00
Tumbler, 6", Footed	22.50

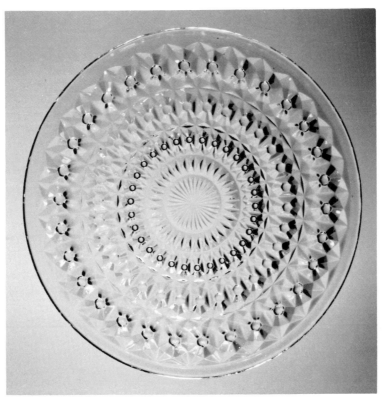

87

HOMESPUN, "FINE RIB"

(pink, crystal)

JEANETTE GLASS COMPANY
1939-1940

New collectors can distinguish Homespun from Hazel Atlas's "Fine Rib" by noticing that Homespun has a waffle-like design in the bottom of its pieces. There is, however, a little variation in the waffle design of the pink and crystal pieces; so don't get upset over that!

If this causes your eyebrow to reach for your hairline, so be it; but I'm beginning to doubt the existence of the 96 ounce pitcher. Further, until a crystal child's tea pot and lid in Homespun show up, I'm going to list the set as a 12 piece child's set.

Presently, one runs into few collectors of Homespun; but it mightn't be a bad idea to round up a few pieces of it anyway simply because it's rather scarcely found and collectors are eventually going to have to turn elsewhere than major patterns! Purses and supply is going to demand it.

The Homespun dinner plate isn't common; nor are large footed 15 ounce tumblers your everyday find. Since I've never found many ash trays, I think it must belong in this list of noticeably short supplied items.

Of course, simply EVERYONE knows that the cups and teapot cover are the tough pieces to find in the child's set. Well, yours truly let a $25.00 set sit at a local flea market — for three months, yet! My very poor reasoning at the time was that one of the cups was chipped and the silly person had the lid sitting on a creamer rather than a teapot; and I didn't wish to be stuck looking high and low for a sugar to go with it anyway. I acknowledge my chagrin when I found out that the set doesn't even have a sugar and creamer! Oh, to have known then what I know now!

	PINK/CRYSTAL
Bowl, 4½", Closed Handles	2.50
Bowl, 5" Cereal	6.50
Bowl, 8¼" Large Berry	6.00
*Butter Dish and Cover	31.50
Coaster/Ash Tray	3.00
Creamer, Footed	2.50
Cup	2.00
Plate, 6" Sherbet	1.00
Plate, 9¼" Dinner	3.00

	PINK/CRYSTAL
Platter, 13" Closed Handles	5.50
Saucer	1.00
Sherbet, Low Flat	1.50
Sugar, Footed	2.50
Tumbler, 4", 9 oz. Water	4.00
Tumbler, 5¼", 13 oz. Iced Tea	6.50
Tumbler, 4", 5 oz. Footed	4.00
Tumbler, 6¼", 9 oz. Footed	5.00
Tumbler, 6½", 15 oz. Footed	9.00

*Crystal: 65.00

HOMESPUN'S CHILD'S TEA SET

	PINK	CRYSTAL		PINK	CRYSTAL
Cup	17.50	12.50	Tea Pot	20.00	
Saucer	6.00	4.75	Tea Pot Cover	30.00	
Plate	8.50	6.50	Set: 14 Pieces	175.00	
			Set: 12 Pieces		125.00

Please refer to Foreword for pricing information

89

INDIANA CUSTARD, "FLOWER AND LEAF BAND"

(ivory or custard, early 1930's, white, 1950's)

INDIANA GLASS COMPANY

If you are searching for a challenge as well as a possible investment for the future, I believe Indiana Custard is a good bet at today's prices. Even if you don't like the color as well as others, you needn't feel lonely in that regard; yet I find that antique dealers will deign to stock this who won't even hear of a piece of that Old Depression Glass being in their shop!

You finally get to see the Indiana Custard decorated saucer in color! I also rounded up a sherbet in Michigan. In all my searching, I've only seen two. Does that tell you anything? It should. They are by far the most difficult pieces to find in this pattern; and the price quoted below may be modest though the ones I've heard of have sold for this.

Butter dishes have actually dropped some on the price scale from last time due to a lack of demand.

Bowls, particularly the oval and the soup bowls, remain in hiding for the most part.

The platter has turned up more often than it used to but not as frequently as collectors would like it to do.

Remember not to sell Indiana Custard short. I believe this pattern may be a sleeper.

FRENCH IVORY	
Bowl, 4⅞" Berry	3.00
Bowl, 5¾" Cereal	3.00
Bowl, 7½" Flat Soup	7.00
Bowl, 8¾" Large Berry	13.50
Bowl, 9½" Oval Vegetable	13.50
Butter Dish and Cover	40.00
Cup	6.00
Creamer	5.50

FRENCH IVORY	
Plate, 5¾" Bread and Butter	2.75
Plate, 7½" Salad	4.00
Plate, 8⅞" Luncheon	5.00
Plate, 9¾" Dinner	6.00
Platter, 11½" Oval	15.00
Saucer	2.25
Sherbet	32.50
Sugar	5.50
Sugar Cover	7.50

91

IRIS, "IRIS AND HERRINGBONE"

(crystal, iridescent, amber) **JEANETTE GLASS COMPANY 1928-1932; 1950; 1970**

Since this Iris candy dish and flat tumbler got left out of the last book, I want you to notice that they are both present now; and for the disbelievers, I have included the little Iris demi-tasse cup and saucers from last year's cover shot. Notice particularly the iridescent which hasn't gotten the recognition it deserves. One ardent collector really wanted it badly enough to call twice and offer more than its worth. Unfortunately for him, this piece is novel enough and small enough to go with me on plane flights for you to see in person at shows.

Again, it is the saucer of the demi-tasse sets that is so hard to find. That's another valuable lesson I learned "later". I saw seven (at one time!) long ago; since then I've bought about thirty cups without saucers.

Everyone who collects Iris, and there are a lot of you who do, is having trouble finding plates especially the 7, 8 and 9 inch ones. The first mentioned is the really tough piece!

I put the Iris coaster up front this year so you could see it easily. It's elusiveness has some people asking me if I've really seen one. Yes! I have.

Some other pieces that collectors are still eager to locate are 5¾ inch goblets and 6 inch cereal bowls. The straight sided six inch Iris cereal is absent from many, many collections.

There seem to be more collectors of crystal Iris; the butter dish and the pitcher are the easy pieces.

In iridescent Iris, due to a reissue in 1969, butter dishes, pitchers, and sugars and creamers are all easily found. No, I don't know of any way to tell the difference between those pieces issued in 1950 and those in 1969. So, don't even worry about that if you collect this pattern. I mean, if you MUST worry, worry that they'll issue it again!

To clear up a few minor questions that have occurred, milk glass vases and candy bottoms were made in the early 1970's. Presently, these pieces are only being made in two tone glass, a red-yellow and a blue-green combination. The molds are slightly different, but the colors are a dead giveaway that these are new.

	CRYSTAL	IRIDESCENT
Bowl, 4½" Berry	2.25	2.50
Bowl, 5" Sauce	2.75	3.00
Bowl, 6" Cereal	5.00	5.00
Bowl, 7½" Soup	10.00	10.50
Bowl, 8" Large Berry	5.00	6.00
Bowl, 9" Salad	5.00	6.00
Bowl, 11" Fruit, 2 Styles	5.00	4.00
Butter Dish and Cover	15.00	17.50
Candlesticks, Pr.	8.00	12.50
Candy Jar and Cover	40.00	
Coaster	17.50	
Creamer, Footed	2.00	3.00
Cup	4.50	4.00
*Demitasse Cup	8.00	20.00
*Demitasse Saucer	12.00	30.00
Goblet, 4" Wine	6.00	6.50
Goblet, 4½" Wine	6.00	

	CRYSTAL	IRIDESCENT	PINK/ GREEN
Goblet, 5¾", 4 oz.	7.50		
Goblet, 5¾", 8 oz.	9.00		
Goblet, 7" Water	9.00		
Pitcher, 9½" Footed	10.00	12.00	
Plate, 5½" Sherbet	1.25	1.50	
Plate, 7" Salad	13.50		
Plate, 8" Luncheon	10.00	5.00	
Plate, 9" Dinner	9.00	6.50	
Plate, 11¾" Sandwich	5.00	6.00	
Saucer	1.00	1.50	
Sherbet, 2½" Footed	4.50	3.50	
Sherbet, 4" Footed	5.50		
Sugar	2.00	3.00	
Sugar Cover	2.00	2.00	
Tumbler, 4" Flat	12.50		
Tumbler, 6" Footed	6.50	5.00	
Tumbler, 7" Footed	8.50	6.00	
Vase, 9"	7.50	9.50	22.50

*Ruby, Blue, Amethyst priced as Iridescent

93

LACE EDGE, "OPEN LACE"

(pink, crystal) HOCKING GLASS COMPANY 1935-1938

Quite a few collectors have jumped on this "Lace edged" bandwagon and as a result, we're beginning to ascertain the scarcity of some pieces. Lace Edge sherbets and tumblers have always been hard to find; but the three legged console bowl and candlesticks in mint condition are beginning to be impossible also.

When I say "mint" condition, that means that the piece is as perfect as it is possible for mass produced, "cheap" glass to be. Perhaps I should say that it means that none of the lacy edges have been cracked, chipped or dinged since this is usually where the problem lies. A damaged piece, even in the rarer items, is worth only about half the price listed for mint pieces depending on the extent of damage. You should not expect to pay, indeed, you should not pay mint prices for damaged merchandise. If you refuse to buy a damaged piece for a high price, then the seller will learn to pick his merchandise better, or better still, will reduce the price to a fair market value for glass that is chipped or damaged. A chip is a chip and the glass is either perfect or not; there is no in-between ground. I bring this whole sermon up in the section under "Pricing" at the front of the book; but this pattern lends itself so well to a soapbox about damaged glass that I couldn't resist; and I've found that some people NEVER read beginning pages of a book no matter how valuable the information contained therein.

You will have to refer to one of my first books to see a picture of the Lace Edge footed tumbler. Frankly, I didn't find one at a reasonable price until after I'd photographed. The rays go only halfway up the tumblers just as they do on the sugar and creamer. Don't confuse them with the Coronation tumblers whose rays climb ⅔ or ¾ the height of the glass.

Notice the Lace Edge cup here also. The rays remain close to the bottom and do not climb the edge of the cup as do those of Queen Mary, the pattern it's usually confused with. You might also note the ribbed bowl on the left. Some bowls lack this ribbing.

You particularly find candlesticks and the console bowl common to dealer's tables in frosted or satin finish pieces. Even at reasonable prices, few people are buying these; so don't go overboard.

The green "Lace Edge" pieces which you see were made by other companies such as Lancaster and Westmoreland. Usually, these are a better quality glass and will "ring" like good glass if you flick an edge with your finger. Our Lace Edge gives a kind of dull thud when done the same way. That's okay. Lace Edge enthusiasts don't collect it for its tonal quality!

	*PINK
**Bowl, 6⅜" Cereal	3.50
Bowl, 7¾" Salad	5.25
Bowl, 9½" Plain or Ribbed	4.50
***Bowl, 10½" 3 Legs	45.00
Butter Dish or Bon Bon With Cover	22.50
***Candlesticks, Pr.	42.50
Candy Jar and Cover, Ribbed	10.50
Comport, 7"	4.50
Comport and Cover, Footed	9.00
Cookie Jar and Cover	15.00
Creamer	7.50
Cup	6.00
Fish Bowl, 1 gal. 8 oz. (Crystal Only)	8.00
Flower Bowl, Crystal Frog (Listed as vase)	5.00

	*PINK
Plate, 7¼" Salad	3.00
Plate, 8¾" Luncheon	3.00
Plate, 10½" Dinner	4.50
Plate, 10½" Grill	3.00
Plate, 13", 3 Part Solid Lace	6.00
Platter, 13¾"	9.00
Platter, 13¾", 5 Part	9.00
Relish Dish, 7½" Deep, 3 Part	4.50
Saucer	3.00
***Sherbet, Footed	22.50
Sugar	7.50
Tumbler, 4½", 9 oz., Flat	5.75
Tumbler, 5", 10½ oz., Footed	15.00

*Satin or frosted items slightly lower in price
**Officially listed as cereal or cream soup
***Price is for absolute mint condition

LAUREL

(French ivory, jade green, white opal and poudre blue)

McKEE GLASS COMPANY
1930's

A number of collectors throughout the country are turning to Laurel; however, the density of collectors seem to be centered mostly in the Ohio-Pennsylvania region where more of it appears.

There seemed to be no way I could improve upon this picture of Laurel taken for the second book, except possibly to find a tumbler. Well, I'm looking at the tumbler NOW; but I had no luck finding it before the photography session. A number of serious collectors have never even seen a tumbler; well, take heart. There seem to be two sizes to look for, the 4½ inch, 9 ounce listed before and a 5 inch, 12 ounce iced tea. Perhaps having two sizes to look for instead of the one will increase your chances of seeing them! At least six of this latter size have shown up.

The poudre blue (that's "powder blue" for you Yankees who didn't take French) and the Scottie Dog items are the elite in Laurel and you will have trouble acquiring these as owners hate to part with them at any price.

French ivory is the most collectible of the usually found colors in Laurel. However, due to the green being less expensive in the past, a number of collectors have turned to it, thus causing a steady rise in price of the green.

When you say that Laurel sherbets, candlesticks, shakers and tumblers are very hard to get, then you may class the three legged console bowl as next to impossible. More collectors will reveal the true scarcity of Laurel.

Many of you are presently limiting yourselves to the already expensive children's items; may I suggest you give thought to a possible better investment in the larger ware which is now cheaper to obtain?

The 7½ inch salad plate is all it takes to make the base of the cheese dish; so don't leave one someplace for lack of an indented bottom. You can find cheese dish tops in every color but blue. Thus far, it's "taken a powder" so to speak.

	WHITE OPAL JADE GREEN	FRENCH IVORY	POUDRE BLUE
Bowl, 5" Berry	2.75	4.00	6.50
Bowl, 6" Cereal	4.00	5.00	8.00
Bowl, 6", Three Legs	6.00	7.50	
Bowl, 9", Large Berry	8.50	12.50	15.00
Bowl, 9¾" Oval Vegetable	12.00	15.00	20.00
Bowl, 10½", Three Legs	20.00	25.00	32.50
Bowl, 11"	15.00	20.00	25.00
Candlesticks, 4", Pr.	15.00	20.00	25.00
Cheese Dish and Cover	40.00	45.00	
Creamer, Short	6.00	7.00	12.50
Creamer, Tall	7.50	8.00	12.50
Cup	4.00	5.00	10.00

	WHITE OPAL JADE GREEN	FRENCH IVORY	POUDRE BLUE
Plate, 6" Sherbet	2.50	3.25	4.00
Plate, 7½" Salad	3.00	5.00	7.50
Plate, 9⅛" Dinner	4.50	5.00	9.00
Plate, 9⅛" Grill	3.00	4.00	7.00
Platter, 10¾" Oval	12.50	15.00	
Salt and Pepper	30.00	30.00	
Saucer	2.00	2.50	4.00
Sherbet	5.75	9.00	
Sugar, Short	6.00	7.00	12.50
Sugar, Tall	7.50	8.00	12.50
Tumbler, 4½", 9 oz. Flat		15.00	
Tumbler, 5", 12 oz. Flat		20.00	

CHILDREN'S LAUREL TEA SET

	PLAIN	DECORATED RIMS	SCOTTY DOG DECAL
Creamer	15.00	25.00	30.00
Cup	12.50	15.00	20.00
Plate	7.50	10.00	15.00
Saucer	5.50	6.50	10.00
Sugar	15.00	25.00	30.00
14 Piece Set	135.00	170.00	250.00

Please refer to Foreword for pricing information

LORAIN, "BASKET", "NO. 615"

(green, yellow, crystal)

INDIANA GLASS COMPANY
1929-1932

An increase in prices of the more difficult to find yellow Lorain has caused me to separate prices by colors.

The most significant jump in price has been made by the 8 inch deep berry bowl in yellow. It's going to leave quite a hole in your personal "basket" should you 'luck into' one! I hope a few of you were able to buy it at last year's $7.00 price tag. You can find this bowl in green, by the way, with a little searching.

Search for the two sizes of Lorain dinner plates continues with that 10¼ inch getting

practically impossible to find in any color. Crystal Lorain is enticing collectors but some give up the quest when they discover how little of it there is to be found.

Another bowl which has seemingly been all grabbed up by collectors is the 6 inch cereal bowl in all colors. Consider yourself lucky if you've latched onto just one in yellow. You may notice the absence of any pictured. I just couldn't turn one up in my wanderings.

There's been no news of a Lorain pitcher. I keep hoping someone will find a full basket of them in someone's old shop as they did with the Parrot pitchers.

	CRYSTAL/ GREEN	YELLOW		CRYSTAL/ GREEN	YELLOW
Bowl, 6" Cereal	2.50	6.00	Plate, 9⅜" Dinner	4.00	4.50
Bowl, 7¼" Salad	4.50	5.00	Plate, 10¼" Dinner	6.00	8.50
Bowl, 8" Deep Berry	9.00	20.00	Plate, 11½" Cake	8.00	12.00
Bowl, 9¾" Oval Vegetable	8.50	9.00	Platter, 11½"	6.50	8.00
Creamer, Footed	3.50	4.00	Relish, 8", 4 Part	4.00	4.00
Cup	2.50	3.00	Saucer	1.50	1.50
Plate, 5½" Sherbet	1.50	1.50	Sherbet, Footed	3.25	4.50
Plate, 7¾" Salad	2.50	2.50	Sugar, Footed	3.50	4.00
Plate, 8⅜" Luncheon	2.50	3.00	Tumbler, 4¾", 9 oz. Footed	5.50	7.00

99

MADRID

(green, pink, amber, crystal, "Madonna" blue) **FEDERAL GLASS COMPANY 1932-1939**

The news Depression Glass collectors feared would happen sooner or later occurred "sooner" when the Federal Glass Company redesigned molds to make their "Recollection" Madrid for the Bi-Centennial. Each of the pieces are marked with a '76 in the design so their intent was not to fool anyone. The color of amber is similar to the old, but if you see them side by side the experienced eye can tell the difference not only by color but by the sharpness of the design of the new. The biggest worry is that some people are putting the new better top on the old butter bottom; so look carefully and don't be fooled. There is a big difference in the knobs on the old and new butter tops. The new mold marks run through the North and South poles of the knob while the old mold marks form an equator around the middle of the knob. The new knob appears to be slightly smaller; but the mold marks are your best means of identification.

For price comparison, here is what the new sells for in stores.

Plate, 11" dinner	4 for $6.00
Plate, 8¼" salad	4 for $4.58
Cup	4 for $3.50
Saucer	4 for $3.50
Bowl, 7½" soup	4 for $4.50
Bowl, 9½" square	$6.00
Bowl, oval vegetable	$6.00
Butter dish and cover	$6.00
20 piece starter set (4 dinners, 4 salads, 4 cups, 4 saucers, 4 soups)	$19.00

It will be tempting to many collectors to fill out the dinner plates to their collection by buying the new Recollection due to the high cost of the old Madrid. However, in my area, the older Madrid has been selling

well while the newer is causing little stir; so one would suppose that collectors still seek the older glass. It is my understanding that some people are buying sets of the new and setting it aside for the future. My personal feeling has been not to purchase it since it cost a small fortune for Federal to remake the molds and I refuse to help them pay for them as encouragement on my part to perhaps make some other pattern in the future. Those are my feelings. You follow your own dictates.

Several items have increased considerably in price from last time, particularly the crystal butter dish and shakers.

Demand for the blue has not been as great as in the past, so the price line has pretty much held in that.

Prices for amber have been steadily rising. Watch for the walnut lazy susan pictured here. They have shown up in West Virginia, Virginia, and eastern Kentucky. Most of the hard to get gravy boats and platters have been turning up in the Iowa area leading one to assume that certain items were limited to distribution in certain regions of the country. By the way, the gravy boat has still only been found in amber. Finding it in another color, especially blue, would feather your nest nicely!

The amber ash tray has turned out to be more scarce than the green. It was the amber one I first discovered at an antique show and had to buy the whole set of dishes to get.

Look for perfect sugar lids in Madrid as they represent a hardship to locate.

	CRYSTAL/ AMBER	PINK	GREEN	BLUE
Ash Tray, 6" Square	45.00		45.00	
Bowl, 4¾" Cream Soup	3.00	*	*	
Bowl, 5" Sauce	1.25	1.50	2.00	4.00
Bowl, 7" Soup	3.00	*	6.00	9.00
Bowl, 8" Salad	6.00	*	9.50	17.50
Bowl, 9⅜" Large Berry	6.00	*		*
Bowl, 9½", Deep Salad	9.00			
Bowl, 10" Oval Vegetable	5.50	8.00	9.00	13.00
††Bowl, 11" Low Console	5.50	6.00		
Butter Dish and Cover	†40.00	*	40.00	*
††Candlesticks, 2¼", Pr.	8.00	10.00	*	*
Cookie Jar and Cover	15.00	17.50	*	*
Creamer, Footed	3.00	5.00	5.00	8.00
Cup	2.75	4.00	4.00	8.00
Gravy Boat and Platter	400.00			
Hot Dish Coaster	17.50	*	20.00	*
Hot Dish Coaster w/Indent	20.00	*	22.50	*
Jam Dish, 7"	5.00		6.50	9.00
Jello Mold, 2⅛" High	3.50		*	
Pitcher, 5½", 36 oz. Juice	15.00	*	*	*
Pitcher, 8", 60 oz. Square	20.00	25.00	95.00	110.00
Pitcher, 8½", 80 oz.	30.00	*	125.00	*

	CRYSTAL/ AMBER	PINK	GREEN	BLUE
Pitcher, 8½", 80 oz. Ice Lip	30.00	*	125.00	*
Plate, 6" Sherbet	1.00	1.75	1.50	3.25
Plate, 7½" Salad	2.50	3.00	3.50	6.00
Plate, 8⅞" Luncheon	2.50	3.00	3.00	6.00
Plate, 10½" Dinner	12.50	12.50	15.00	15.00
Plate, 10½" Grill	3.00		5.00	*
Plate, 10¼" Relish	5.00	5.00	7.50	
††Plate, 11¼" Cake Round	4.25	4.50	6.00	*
Platter, 11½" Oval	4.00	6.50	8.00	11.50
Salt/Pepper, 3½", Footed	30.00	*	42.50	85.00
Salt/Pepper, 3½", Flat	22.50	*	32.50	*
Saucer	1.00	1.00	1.50	3.00
Sherbet, Two Styles	3.00		4.50	7.00
Sugar	2.50	3.00	3.00	8.00
Sugar Cover	12.50	15.00	15.00	25.00
Tumbler, 3⅞", 5 oz.	7.00			12.00
Tumbler, 4¼", 9 oz.	6.50	8.00	12.50	11.50
Tumbler, 5½", 12 oz., 2 Styles	9.00	*	15.00	14.00
Tumbler, 4", 5 oz. Footed	11.50	*	27.50	*
Tumbler 5½", 10 oz. Footed	12.50	*	17.50	*
Wooden Lazy Susan, 7 Hot Dish Coasters	275.00			

Please refer to Foreword for pricing information

†Crystal — $200.00
†† (Iridescent priced slightly higher)

100

*Item should exist as listed in old catalogs or other publications but can not be confirmed by author.

MANHATTAN, "HORIZONTAL RIBBED"

(pink, crystal, green)

ANCHOR HOCKING GLASS COMPANY
1939-1941

Manhattan still ranks as a good set for beginning collectors to gather. It's easy to spot, durable to use and it will not cost an arm and a leg to purchase. Pink remains the most desirable color; but it's also harder to locate. Crystal isn't as plentiful as it once was due to more and more of it finding its way into collections.

The Manhattan lazy susan pictured was actually sold with ruby sections. You can also find it with crystal and pink insets; but the ruby seem to catch a better gleam in the collector's eye.

No one has yet found a Manhattan green

pitcher to go with the tumbler pictured. You

see tumblers pretty often; so there must be a pitcher!

You won't see many of the small pink 42 ounce pitchers.

Though you will find other candle holders that seem to blend with the pattern, the square 4½ inch one pictured is the actual one listed by Hocking.

The little wine, again, fits well with the pattern; but no information has yet surfaced to make it genuine Manhattan.

	CRYSTAL	PINK
Ashtray, 4″	.75	1.75
Bowl, 4½″ Sauce	.75	1.25
Bowl, 5⅜″ Berry		
With Handles	.75	1.25
Bowl, 7½″ Large Berry	2.00	3.50
Bowl, 8″ Closed Handles	2.00	3.50
Bowl, 9″ Salad	3.50	7.00
Bowl, 9½″ Fruit	3.50	8.00
Candlesticks, 4½″		
(Double) Pr.	5.00	10.00
Candy Dish, 3 Legs	1.75	2.50
Coaster, 3½″	1.00	1.50
Comport, 5¾″	1.25	2.50
Creamer, Oval	1.25	2.50
Cup	1.00	2.00
Relish Tray, 14″, 4 Part	2.50	4.00

	CRYSTAL	PINK
Relish Tray, 14″, 5 Part	3.50	6.00
Pitcher, 42 oz.	4.50	7.50
Pitcher, 80 oz. Tilted	5.50	12.50
Plate, 6″ Sherbet	.75	1.25
Plate, 8½″ Salad	1.25	1.75
Plate, 10¼″ Dinner	1.75	3.00
Plate, 14″ Sandwich	2.00	4.00
Salt/Pepper, 2″, Pr.		
(Square)	4.00	17.50
Saucer	.75	1.25
Sherbet	1.00	2.00
Sugar, Oval	1.25	2.50
* Tumbler, 10 oz. Footed	2.50	4.50
Vase, 8″	3.00	6.00
Wine, 3½″	5.00	

*Green — $4.50

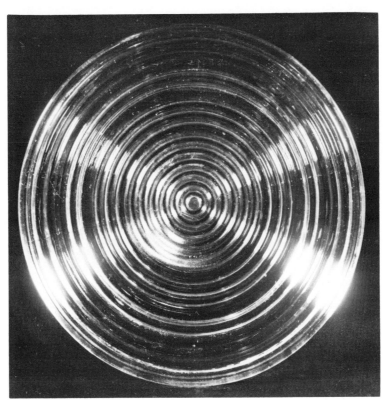

103

MAYFAIR

(crystal, amber, green)

FEDERAL GLASS COMPANY
1934

Mayfair by Federal was redesigned into the Rosemary pattern after only a short issue. For those of you who don't know the story, it was redesigned when it was found that Hocking already had the name "Mayfair" patented. Frankly, it looks like it would have been just as simple to change the name; but Federal chose to change the pattern.

You can see pieces in the photograph that reflect the transitional period between the two patterns of Mayfair and Rosemary. The cream soups and the tumbler are all a part of the transition as well as the green cup and sugar and the amber creamer on the far right. The panels between the flowers are plain on these. If you flip over to Rosemary, you can see what design was arrived at for that pattern. As there are no arches along the base of the Rosemary pieces, I am inclined to include the transitional pieces with the Mayfair pattern rather than with Rosemary. Personally, I would like to make

a whole new pattern of these transitional pieces; but as there are so few pieces, that's rather pointless. Too, since the transitional items with the arches are a lot more rare than Rosemary ones without arches, they fit in more nearly with the rarer Mayfair prices than they do with Rosemary. Thus, they are priced within the Mayfair pattern.

The best way to collect Federal Mayfair is by carrying a rabbit's foot and a four leaf clover and wearing your "lucky" shirt or blouse. You'll need all the help you can get. Prices do not yet reflect how rare this glass is; luckily for us, they may never reflect its true scarcity since so little is available to even get collectors interested in it.

The only item you will encounter with any frequency is a green Mayfair tumbler. Yes, it would be a good pattern to "squirrel away".

	AMBER	CRYSTAL	GREEN
Bowl, 5" Sauce	3.00	2.75	4.00
Bowl, 5" Cream Soup	12.50	7.50	12.00
Bowl, 6" Cereal	5.50	3.00	6.00
Bowl, 10" Oval Vegetable	10.00	5.50	12.00
Creamer, Footed	5.00	4.00	6.00
Cup	4.25	3.00	5.00
Plate, 6¾" Salad	2.00	1.75	3.00
Plate, 9½" Dinner	4.50	3.00	5.00
Plate, 9½" Grill	4.50	3.50	5.50
Platter, 12" Oval	10.00	6.50	12.00
Saucer	1.75	1.00	1.75
Sugar, Footed	5.00	4.00	6.00
Tumbler, 4½", 9 oz.	9.00	6.00	9.00

MAYFAIR, "OPEN ROSE"

(pink, green, blue, yellow, crystal)

HOCKING GLASS COMPANY

1931-1937

There have been a number of significant new finds in this most popular of Depression patterns. Unfortunately, nearly all came after we photographed.

Even if it didn't grace the cover or the rare page, I hope you will appreciate the separate photographing of the Mayfair footed shaker. That seemed just too good to pass up until "next time". It came from an auction in Ohio to Kentucky ; and when I heard it was only fifty miles away, I missed a day of teaching to try and round it up. It's a bachelor so far, very interested in finding a mate, I might add!

When I listed only six known sugar lids in pink Mayfair before, I didn't realize how many reports I would get on the seventh one! I got sixteen letters during the year reporting the seventh though only eleven turned out to be the genuine article. On top of that, I have seen four others. So, when you couple that with the reports received at various shows, there appear to be at least thirty now known. The price quoted below represents what several have sold for. I've heard of both higher and lower prices; but I know they will sell for this if they are perfect and if someone who collects the pattern has the money to spend. It seems quite a lot to spend for a sugar lid when you consider the number that have turned up lately over the country.

New pieces have arrived on the scene in those glorious green and yellow Mayfair colors which we photographed in the second edition. The 9 inch divided celery shown last in green has been found in yellow Mayfair along with a yellow 8 inch, 60 ounce pitcher, a 6 inch plate, and last but not least, a complete yellow Mayfair butter dish! In green, a 4 3/4 inch sherbet has surfaced. Unfortunately, my green Mayfair butter lid is still finding it drafty going around bottomless. But I have hope; for after showing the top to the green candy last year, a bottom was found for it. May this trend continue!

Frosted or satin finish pieces of Mayfair are being discovered in nearly every item. These were made at the factory and many were hand painted with flowers. Dishwashers and very hot dish water are causing havoc with these flowers, however. The frosted finish won't come off, but the flowers will. In general, the frosted items bring from twenty to fifty per cent less than the regular items due to a lack of demand for them. Dealers I've queried tell me that there are a few collectors of frosted items, but they are few and far between.

Dinner plates, cream soups and the tall footed iced tea glasses in pink Mayfair which were formerly readily available are beginning to disappear from view. A new item just discovered in pink is a 5¼ inch goblet which holds 4½ ounces.

More and more collectors are turning to the blue Mayfair in spite of the higher prices simply because it is one of the most strikingly beautiful colors to be found in any of the Depression patterns.

One word of caution. Crystal Mayfair brings about half the price of the pink. Yet some unscrupulous few are taking crystal shakers and dying them blue by putting Rit inside. Thus, in these dark cornered shops, for lack of anything better, a sputum test might be in order as this "applied" color washes off.

	*PINK	BLUE	GREEN	YELLOW
Bowl, 5" Cream Soup	11.50			
Bowl, 5½" Cereal	4.00	12.00		20.00
Bowl, 7" Vegetable	7.00	22.50	45.00	45.00
Bowl, 9", 3⅛" High, 3 Leg Console	500.00			
Bowl, 9½", Oval Vegetable	5.50	19.00	50.00	55.00
Bowl, 10" Vegetable	8.00	20.00		
Bowl, 10" Same Covered	20.00	35.00		
Bowl, 11¾" Low Flat	8.50	31.00	10.00	60.00
Bowl, 12" Deep Scalloped Fruit	8.50	30.00	10.00	60.00
Butter Dish and Cover or				
7" Covered Vegetable	25.00	150.00	300.00	300.00
Cake Plate, 10" Footed	7.00	23.50	35.00	
Candy Dish and Cover	13.00	65.00	285.00	285.00
Celery Dish, 9", Divided			75.00	75.00
**Celery Dish 10" or 10" Divided	7.00	17.50	40.00	40.00
Cookie Jar and Lid	12.00	60.00	250.00	
Creamer, Footed	6.00	20.00	60.00	60.00
Cup	4.50	19.00	40.00	40.00
Decanter and Stopper, 32 oz.	45.00			
Goblet, 3¾", 1 oz. Liquer	125.00		175.00	
Goblet, 4" Cocktail, 3½ oz.	27.50			
Goblet, 4½" Wine, 3 oz.	30.00			
Goblet, Claret, 5¼", 4½ oz.	175.00			
Goblet, 5¾" Water, 9 oz.	17.50			
Goblet, 7¼" Thin, 9 oz.	42.50	40.00		
Pitcher, 6", 37 oz.	12.00	35.00		200.00
Pitcher, 8", 60 oz.	15.00	50.00	200.00	200.00
Pitcher, 8½", 80 oz.	22.00	75.00	250.00	250.00
Plate, 6"				
(Often Substituted as Saucer)	2.00	5.00	15.00	15.00

	*PINK	BLUE	GREEN	YELLO
Plate, 6½" Round Sherbet	3.00			
Plate, 6½" Round, Off Center Indent	10.00	12.50	35.00	
Plate, 8½" Luncheon	4.75	10.00		40
Plate, 9½" Dinner	15.00	17.50		50
Plate, 9½" Grill	7.00	12.50		
Plate, 12" Cake W/Handles	7.50	19.00	9.00	
Platter, 12" Oval, Open Handles	7.50	17.50	85.00	85
Platter, 12½" Oval				
Closed Handles, 8" Wide				135
Relish, 8⅜", 4 part or Non-Partitioned	7.00	22.50	85.00	85
Salt and Pepper, Pr., Flat	22.00	95.00		325
Salt and Pepper, Pr., Footed	700.00			
Sandwich Server/Center Handle	9.00	27.50	9.00	65
Saucer (Cup Ring)	6.25			
Saucer (See 6" Plate)				
Sherbet, 2¼" Flat	25.00	25.00	47.50	
Sherbet, 3" Footed	4.75			
Sherbet, 4¾" Footed	25.00	25.00	95.00	95
Sugar, Footed	6.00	20.00	60.00	60
Sugar Lid	300.00			
Tumbler, 3½", 5 oz. Juice	12.50	37.50		
Tumbler, 4¼", 9 oz. Water	12.00	32.00		
Tumbler, 4¾", 11 oz. Water	13.50	40.00		
Tumbler, 5¼", 13½ oz. Iced Tea	15.00	40.00		
Tumbler, 3¼", 3 oz. Footed Juice	35.00			
Tumbler, 5¼", 10 oz. Footed	10.00	35.00		95
Tumbler, 6½", 15 oz. Ftd. Iced Tea	16.50	37.50	105.00	
Vase, (Sweet Pea)	27.50	25.00	60.00	
Whiskey, 2¼", 1½ oz.	45.00			

*Frosted or satin finish items slightly lower
**Divided Pink Celery — $20.00

Please refer to Foreword for pricing information

MISS AMERICA

(pink, green, crystal, blue)

HOCKING GLASS COMPANY
1933-1937

If the prices for the pink butter dish continue to spiral, pretty soon finding a Miss America butter is going to about equal winning said title! Do remember that the prices are for MINT CONDITION butter dishes. The butter dish in mint condition IS rare. Since, however, most tops are nicked, or chunked, you must be mindful of the fact that spent monies won't replace lost chips. The better condition your piece of expensive glass is in, the more easily you can sell it should the occasion arise. Naturally, if you find a top to the butter for a quarter and it has some nicks, you're not hurt; however, if you pay two hundred dollars for the same piece, you may have a problem.

Goblets, tumblers and shakers continue the upward price trend, but more so in pink than in crystal although the prices of crystal are increasing too, just not as fast. I stand by my statement that the crystal butter is far more scarce than the pink. I have owned three times as many pink as crystal butter dishes. Notice the original sticker on the pink butter!

The only new piece of pink to emerge is a divided relish like the one shown in crystal.

The ice blue dinner plate and sherbet plates continue to be conversation pieces since too few have shown up to create any demand.

I kept the red goblet to remind me of the days when I turned down four. Fifty dollars sounded like a whale of a lot of money then!

I almost had a great coup for the book when I purchased a platter, dinner plate, saucer and several other pieces in green! When it arrived, I could see streaks where the color had already come off. If the color is fired on, naval jelly won't take it off; if someone has simply sprayed some color on, it will dissolve. Yet, I am haunted by the almost certainty of having seen a saucer in "true" green and a small berry dish in pink in my past travels; so I'm not going to be all that surprised when someone finds them. While in Denver, I did see one green shaker; so be on the lookout for its mate.

The list of items here are from Hocking's old catalogues; so if you have a piece which looks like Miss America but isn't in this listing, try checking under English Hobnail pattern as the two are often confused.

	CRYSTAL	PINK	GREEN	RED
Bowl, 4½" Berry			6.00	
*Bowl, 6¼" Berry	3.00	4.00	8.00	
Bowl, 8" Curved in at top	20.00	25.00		200.00
Bowl, 8¾" Straight Deep Fruit	17.50	22.50		
Bowl, 10" Oval Vegetable	5.00	9.00		
**Butter Dish and Cover	175.00	325.00		
Cake Plate, 12" Footed	10.00	15.00		
Candy Jar and Cover, 11½"	37.50	50.00		
Celery Dish, 10½" Oblong	4.00	6.50		
Coaster, 5¾"	10.00	15.00		
Comport, 5"	6.00	7.50		
Creamer, Footed	3.50	6.50		95.00
Cup	4.50	6.50	7.00	
Goblet, 3¾", 3 oz. Wine	13.50	30.00		110.00
Goblet, 4¾", 5 oz. Juice	12.00	25.00		110.00
Goblet, 5½", 10 oz. Water	13.00	17.50		110.00
Pitcher, 8", 65 oz. W/Ice Lip	40.00	55.00		
Pitcher, 8½", 65 oz. W/Ice Lip	45.00	57.50		

	CRYSTAL	PINK	GREEN	RED
***Plate, 5¾" Sherbet	2.00	3.25	5.00	
Plate, 6¾"			6.00	
Plate, 8½" Salad	2.75	6.00	7.00	50.00
****Plate, 10½" Dinner	5.00	9.00	7.00	
Plate, 10¼" Grill	4.00	5.50	7.00	
Platter, 12" Oval	6.50	10.00	7.00	
Relish, 8¾", 4 Part	3.50	8.00	7.00	
Relish, 11¾" Round Divided	8.00	15.00	7.00	
Salt and Pepper, Pr.	17.00	23.00	250.00	
Saucer	1.50	2.50		
Sherbet	3.00	5.25		
Sugar	3.50	6.50		95.00
Tid-Bit, 2 Tier, 8½" and 10¼" Plates	18.00	27.50		
Tumbler, 4", 5 oz. Juice	7.50	20.00		
Tumbler, 4½", 10 oz. Water	8.00	13.00	13.50	
Tumbler, 6¾", 14 oz. Iced Tea	12.00	22.50		

*Also has appeared in Cobalt Blue — $75.00
**Absolute mint price
***Also in Ice Blue — $25.00
****Also in Ice Blue — $50.00

Please refer to Foreword for pricing information

MODERNTONE, "WEDDING BAND"

(blue, amethyst platonite fired-on colors, pink, crystal)

HAZEL ATLAS GLASS COMPANY
1934-1942

Simplicity of pattern as well as the amethyst and cobalt colors attracts collectors to Moderntone. Several people have told me that they received luncheon sets of this as wedding gifts. Their friends were suiting its "name" to the occasion, no doubt.

The 9 ounce tumbler and the little 1½ ounce whiskey have only been found in cobalt so far. These tumblers were made by Hazel Atlas and are being used with this pattern although nothing officially naming them as Moderntone has been found. Too, until I see a 5 ounce or a 12 ounce tumbler, I'm not going to include them.

I mentioned the cheese dish and the ash tray before; now you can see them. Only a few cheese dishes have cropped up, but each has had the wooden cutting board included.

Pictured is one style of sugar cover and a couple of the many butter tops being found or being put on the butter bottoms. The factory, itself, didn't issue any butter tops; so who is to say which is the proper one.

I have found a crystal sugar and a transparent pink creamer in Moderntone which could indicate a small issue of items in these colors.

I'm certain it took someone several hours to round up all these fired-on shakers. I will list the "platonite" (fired-on) colors this time; but I suspect you can find colored items for even less than I have them listed.

	COBALT	AMETHYST	PLATONITE FIRED ON COLORS		COBALT	AMETHYST	PLATONITE FIRED ON COLORS
*Ash Tray, 7¾", Match Holder in Center	62.50			Plate, 5¾" Sherbet	1.00	1.25	.50
				Plate, 6¾" Salad	1.25	1.50	.75
Bowl, 4¾" Cream Soup	2.75	3.50		Plate, 7¾" Luncheon	1.75	2.50	1.00
Bowl, 5" Berry	2.50	2.50	.50	Plate, 8⅞" Dinner	2.50	3.00	1.25
Bowl, 5" Cream Soup	3.50	4.00	1.00	Plate, 10½" Sandwich	6.00	6.00	1.75
Bowl, 6½" Cereal	4.50	4.50	.75	Platter, 11" Oval	6.00	7.00	1.50
Bowl, 7½" Soup	6.50	7.50	1.00	Platter, 12" Oval	7.00	8.00	1.50
Bowl, 8¾" Large Berry	8.00	10.00	2.00	Salt and Pepper, Pr.	12.50	17.50	5.50
Butter Dish With Metal Cover	45.00			Saucer	1.00	1.25	.50
Cheese Dish, 7" With Metal Lid	57.50			Sherbet	2.00	2.50	1.25
				Sugar	2.75	3.50	1.25
Creamer	2.75	3.50	1.25	Sugar Lid in Metal	12.50		
Cup	1.75	2.00	.75	Tumbler, 5 oz.			1.00
Cup (Handle-less) or Custard	3.00	4.00		Tumbler, 9 oz.	4.00		1.00
				Tumbler, 12 oz.			1.50
				Whiskey, 1½ oz.	3.00		1.00

*Pink — $75.00

MOONDROPS

(amber, pink, green, cobalt blue, ice blue, red, amethyst, crystal,

dark green, light green, jadite, smoke, black)

NEW MARTINSVILLE

1932-1940's

If the picture for Moondrops looks a little jammed, just take a look at the color listing and maybe you'll see why! All colors known are shown save for the black which has only been seen in tumblers thus far. The owner couldn't part with even one of those for me to show them. Perhaps it's just as well. Where would I have put it?

If nothing else caught your eye on the cover, the etched amber Moondrops butterdish with the underplate should have. There are six of these hard to find butter dishes shown. Only the crystal butter will not break the $200.00 price listed. The red and cobalt colors should bring more.

For the time being, I will not try to separate this multitude of colors and I'm listing only the pieces known to me in sizes as I measured them. You may be certain that the red color will bring about 20 percent more than the price listed for the group and the crystal will bring about that much less. The red is most in demand; but other colors are much more rarely found.

In my area, the cobalt will bring about the same as the red.

Let's discuss some of the "nicknames" for the styles shown. There are four decanters, a small, medium and large, plus the pink "rocket" style shown; notice the tripod stand, cone and "engine". There are two styles of stoppers, a "beehive" and a "fan tail". There's a "rocket" pink wine shown in front of the pink butter dish and an amber "rocket" perfume by the green pitcher.

The ice blue candlestick represents the "winged" style; a "winged" console bowl is also available.

In amethyst you can see both the ruffled candle (left) and the sherbet style (right). The blue covered bowl we're calling a casserole; it could be a candy if you so desire.

The sugar and creamer shown on the tray are the miniature size.

	ALL COLORS		ALL COLORS
Ash Tray	6.00	Goblet, 6¼", Water, 9 oz.	9.50
Bowl, 5¼", Berry	3.00	Mug, 5⅛", 12 oz.	12.00
Bowl, 6¾", Soup	5.00	Perfume Bottle, "rocket"	15.00
Bowl, 7½", Pickle	7.50	Pitcher, Small, 6⅞", 22 oz.	60.00
Bowl, 8⅜", Footed, Concave Top	10.00	Pitcher, Medium, 8⅛", 32 oz.	75.00
Bowl, 8½", Three Footed, Divided Relish	8.00	Pitcher, Large With Lip, 8", 50 oz.	90.00
Bowl, 9½", Three Legged, Ruffled	10.00	Pitcher, Large, No Lip, 8⅛", 53 oz.	90.00
Bowl, 9¾", Oval Vegetable	12.00	Plate, 5⅞", Bread and Butter	1.50
Bowl, 9¾", Covered Casserole	30.00	Plate, 6⅛", Sherbet	1.50
Bowl, 9¾", Two Handled, Oval	20.00	Plate, 6" Round, Off-Center Indent for Sherbet	3.00
Bowl, 11½", Celery, Boat Shaped	12.50	Plate, 7⅛", Salad	2.00
Bowl, 12", Three Footed, Round Console	15.00	Plate, 8½" Luncheon	2.00
Bowl, 13", Console with "wings"	17.50	Plate, 9½" Dinner	4.50
Butter Dish and Cover	200.00	Plate, 15" Round Sandwich	8.00
Candles, 2", Ruffled, Pr.	15.00	Plate, 15", Two Handled Sandwich	8.50
Candles, 4½", Sherbet Style, Pr.	12.50	Platter, 12" Oval	10.00
Candlesticks, 5", "wings", Pr.	20.00	Saucer	1.75
Candlesticks, 5¼", Triple Light, Pr.	25.00	Sherbet, 2⅝"	5.00
Candlesticks, 8½", Metal Stem, Pr.	17.50	Sherbet, 4½"	7.50
Candy Dish, 8", Ruffled	9.00	Sugar, 2¾"	7.00
Cocktail Shaker, with or without handle, metal top	12.50	Sugar, 4"	5.00
Comport, 4"	5.00	Tumbler, 2¾", Shot, 2 oz.	5.50
Comport, 11½"	11.00	Tumbler, 2¾", Handled Shot, 2 oz.	6.00
Creamer, 2¾", Miniature	7.00	Tumbler, 3¼", Footed Juice, 3 oz.	6.50
Creamer, 3¾", Regular	5.00	Tumbler, 3⅝", 5 oz.	5.00
Cup	4.00	Tumbler, 4⅜", 7 oz.	7.00
Decanter, Small, 7¾"	22.50	Tumbler, 4⅜", 8 oz.	8.00
Decanter, Medium, 8½"	27.50	Tumbler, 4⅞", Handled, 9 oz.	9.00
Decanter, Large, 11¼"	32.50	Tumbler, 4⅞", 9 oz.	9.00
Decanter, "rocket", 10¼"	45.00	Tumbler, 5⅛", 12 oz.	9.50
Goblet, 2⅞", ¾ oz. Liquer	10.00	Tray, 7½", For Miniature Sugar/Creamer	9.00
Goblet, 4", 4 oz. Wine	7.50	Vase, 7¾", Flat, Ruffled Top	30.00
Goblet, 4¼", "rocket" Wine	10.00	Vase, 9¼", "rocket" style	45.00
Goblet, 4¾", 5 oz.	6.00		
Goblet, 5⅛", Metal Stem Wine	6.00		
Goblet, 5½", Metal Stem Wine	7.00		

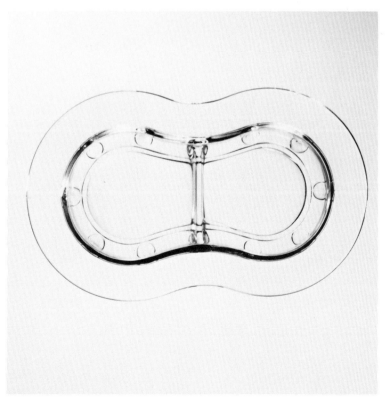

MOONSTONE
(crystal with opalescent hobnails)

ANCHOR HOCKING GLASS COMPANY
1941-1946

Technically, this isn't Depression Glass as many a World War II couple set their tables with it. However, it is being eagerly collected and is here out of popular demand. Sometimes this pattern is confused with older glass because of its opalescent effect.

Since I had so many requests to identify by location the pieces shown, I'll make the attempt. I think most of the confusion came because the cloverleaf open candy was missing from the last price listing though it was in the photo; I hope with its inclusion now to make each piece recognizeable. "Crimping" refers to the ruffled edges of the pieces.

There are four size bowls on the right that are crimped. The medium sized 7¾" bowl is shown divided or non-divided. The 5½ inch dessert is in front of those medium bowls

and the larger, 9½ inch vegetable bowl is behind. The candy dish is positioned in the rear left; the cigarette box is the rectangular covered box at front right and the puff box is the round, covered dish at center left. Identification of the remaining pieces should be easy for you.

It's possible to find other opalescent hobnail items made by other companies, Fenton Glass Company in particular. However, if your piece isn't among those listed here, it's probably not Moonstone. On flat pieces, Moonstone has raised rays in the base with one set of hobnails inside the base ring.

This is another of the less expensive sets to collect and one that is, perhaps, more attractive than the inexpensive crystal patterns.

	OPALESCENT HOBNAIL
Bowl, 5½" Berry	2.00
Bowl, 5½" Crimped Dessert	3.00
Bowl, 6½" Crimped, Handled	3.75
Bowl, 7¾" Flat	4.25
Bowl, 7¾" Divided Relish	4.00
Bowl, 9½" Crimped	7.50
Bowl, Cloverleaf	6.00
Candleholder, Pr.	8.50
Candy Jar and Cover, 6"	8.00
Cigarette Jar and Cover	7.00
Creamer	3.00

	OPALESCENT HOBNAIL
Cup	3.00
Goblet, 10 oz.	6.00
Heart Bonbon, One Handle	4.75
Plate, 6¼" Sherbet	1.50
Plate, 8" Luncheon	4.00
Plate, 10" Sandwich	7.00
Puff Box and Cover, 4¾", Round	8.00
Saucer (Same as Sherbet Plate)	1.50
Sherbet, Footed	4.00
Sugar, Footed	3.00
Vase, 5½" Bud	5.50

Please refer to Foreword for pricing information

MT. PLEASANT, "DOUBLE SHIELD"

(black, cobalt blue, green, pink)

L. E. SMITH COMPANY
1920's-1934

Mt. Pleasant was an expensive glass when it was issued as compared to the cheaper or "free when you purchase . . ." glass in other patterns. Thus, you are more likely to find this in antique shops than at the local flea market. It is referred to as "double shield" because of the shield-like design found on the handled items and on the underside of the plate. The "double" business comes from the fact that the shield appears as it would if it were being reflected in a mirror or pool of water, the bottom "shield" being upside down.

Two basic shapes appear, a squarish shape with scalloped-like edges and a round with alternating scallops and points.

You may notice that I added pink to the color listing at the top. I found a pink creamer recently. Who knows what other colors may appear.

I haven't been able to find a complete listing of the pieces in this pattern; doubtless you will find others. One dealer in New York wrote me to say he had twelve other pieces in his extensive collection and he promised to send me a listing. I hope to include those next time. The problem occurs in knowing what to include in this pattern as L. E. Smith made a lot of black glass. I even have a large square bowl with the double shield on it that is decorated with silk screened dogwood blossoms. Is it Mt. Pleasant or some other Dogwood pattern? I hope to find better answers in the future since I should have more time to pursue them. (Nine years of grading papers seemed like enough; so I've joined those veritable legions of "former school teachers".)

	PINK, EBONY, GREEN	BLACK AMETHYST, AMETHYST, COBALT
Bon Bon, Rolled Up Handles	8.00	12.00
Bowl, 3 Footed, Rolled-In Edges, As Rose Bowl	10.00	14.00
Bowl, 8" Scalloped, Two Handles	9.00	13.00
Bowl, 8" Two Handled Square	9.00	13.00
Candlesticks, Single Stem, Pr.	10.00	12.50
Candlesticks, Double Stem, Pr.	14.00	20.00
Creamer (Waffle-like Crystal)	4.00	
Creamer (Scalloped Edges)	6.50	8.50
Cup (Waffle-like Crystal)	2.50	

	PINK, EBONY, GREEN	BLACK AMETHYST, AMETHYST, COBALT
Cup	3.50	5.50
Plate, 8" Scalloped or Square	5.00	8.00
Plate, 8" Solid Handles	6.00	9.00
Plate, 10½" Cake with Solid Handles	10.00	15.00
Salt and Pepper Shakers (Two Styles)	13.00	17.50
Saucer, Square or Scalloped	2.00	2.25
Sherbet, Scalloped Edges	4.00	7.75
Sugar (Waffle-like Crystal)	4.00	
Sugar (Scalloped Edges)	6.50	8.50

NEW CENTURY, and incorrectly, "LYDIA RAY"

(pink, green, crystal, amethyst, cobalt)

HAZEL ATLAS GLASS COMPANY
1930-1935

The name issued by Hazel Atlas for this pattern was New Century and is not to be confused with the Ovide pattern. Turn to Ovide now and see how distinctly different these two patterns are. It's just that the names have been incorrectly interchanged in the past.

This year I was about to list the ash tray as occurring only in crystal until I ran into a green one. Correctly, this is an ash tray/coaster as there is an indent for the glass in the bottom of the tray, something I overlooked when I found the crystal ash tray a few years ago.

This is another pattern in which dinner plates are difficult to locate; so are the grill plates.

The crystal wine was the only one I could find for the picture; and the casserole I ordered for the picture came with the top intact but the bottom shattered into a thousand pieces. Notice the colored rings around the little shot glass as this is rather different. I've seen an advertisement for a green shot glass.

Notice that the pitcher comes with or without the ice lip. There are four pitchers, each style having two sizes.

If you are a novice at collecting Depression Glass, I would leave this pattern to the advanced collectors simply because you could become easily discouraged by not finding it. Now, if you happen onto a big batch of it to start with, then by all means pursue it.

So far, the pink, amethyst and cobalt colors have only been accounted for in pitchers and tumblers. Maybe you could find a piece in something besides the flat tumbler to make your day!

	GREEN, CRYSTAL	PINK, COBALT, AMETHYST
Ash Tray/Coaster, 5⅜"	17.50	
Bowl, 4½" Berry	2.00	
Bowl, 4¾" Cream Soup	6.00	
Bowl, 8" Large Berry	7.50	
Bowl, 9" Covered Casserole	27.50	
Butter Dish and Cover	37.50	
Cup	2.50	
Creamer	4.00	
Decanter and Stopper	25.00	
Goblet, 2½ oz. Wine	7.00	
Goblet, 3¼ oz. Cocktail	8.00	
Pitcher, 7¾", 60 oz., with or without Ice Lip	17.50	18.50
Pitcher, 8", 80 oz., with or without Ice Lip	20.00	25.00
Plate, 6" Sherbet	1.50	

	GREEN CRYSTAL	PINK, COBALT, AMETHYST
Plate, 7⅛" Breakfast	3.00	
Plate, 8½" Salad	3.00	
Plate, 10" Dinner	3.75	
Plate, 10" Grill	4.00	
Platter, 11" Oval	6.00	
Salt and Pepper, Pr.	17.50	
Saucer	1.50	
Sherbet, 3"	4.00	
Sugar	4.00	
Sugar Cover	4.00	
Tumbler, 3½", 5 oz.	4.00	4.50
Tumbler, 4⅛", 9 oz.	5.00	5.50
Tumbler, 5", 10 oz.	5.50	7.00
Tumbler, 5¼", 12 oz.	8.00	8.00
Tumbler, 4", 5 oz. Footed	6.00	
Tumbler, 4⅞", 9 oz. Footed	7.00	
Whiskey, 2½", 1½ oz.	5.00	

Please refer to Foreword for pricing information

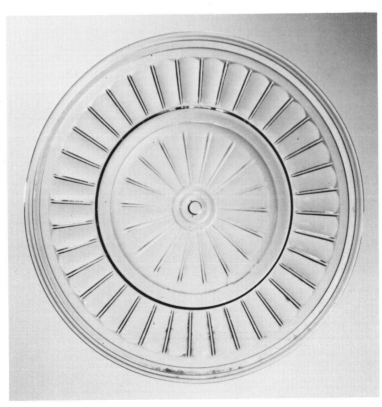

119

NEWPORT, "HAIRPIN"

(cobalt blue, amethyst, pink, "Platonite" white and fired on colors)

HAZEL ATLAS GLASS COMPANY
1936-1940

Collectors are drawn to Newport via its colors of cobalt and amethyst.

By its absence from the picture, you may conclude that the cobalt or amethyst platter is hard to find. The serving pieces in said colors are not all that common either, so look out for them. Other elusive pieces in these colors are tumblers and all sizes of bowls.

There are two shades of white. In the shaker at the left, you see a kind of opalescent white; while the one on the right has a white similar to a heavier milk glass color. You shouldn't encounter this often, but I have noticed it in several pieces; so if you are interested in this color, you had better watch for this slightly bothersome trait as the two colors do not match up all that well.

Newport shakers can be used as substitutes for those missing in monax Petalware. In fact, they are often incorrectly called "Petalware" shakers.

The platonite colors were fired on over white, but few people have shown any interest in collecting these as yet.

	*COBALT	AMETHYST		*COBALT	AMETHYST
Bowl, 4¼" Berry	2.00	2.50	Plate, 11½" Sandwich	9.50	11.50
Bowl, 4¾" Cream Soup	5.00	6.00	Platter, 11¾" Oval	9.50	11.50
Bowl, 5¼" Cereal	2.00	2.50	Salt and Pepper	15.00	17.50
Bowl, 8¼" Large Berry	8.00	10.00	Saucer	1.50	1.75
Cup	2.25	2.75	Sherbet	3.50	4.00
Creamer	3.00	3.50	Sugar	3.00	3.50
Plate, 6" Sherbet	1.50	1.75	Tumbler, 4½", 9 oz.	7.00	8.00
Plate, 8½" Luncheon	3.25	3.50			

*WHITE 60% of Cobalt price

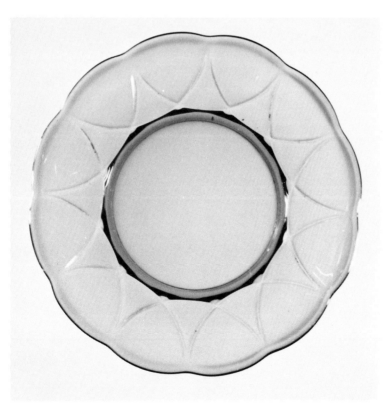

NORMANDIE, "BOUQUET AND LATTICE"

(iridescent, amber, pink, crystal)

FEDERAL GLASS COMPANY

1933-1940

Collectors are having difficulties in completing sets in either pink or amber Normandie. I haven't yet met a collector of the iridescent, but there is plenty of that yet to be bought. The only hitch might come in talking some antique dealers out of the "rare" twenty dollar "carnival" plates or the twenty-five dollar cup and saucer. The iridescent is not Carnival Glass and it is by no means rare.

Normandie sugar lids in both amber and pink are few and far between, with those in pink being a bit fewer and farther between. Collecting pink has been catching on more than collecting amber in some circles though

finding pink shakers or a pink juice tumbler may take some doing. The oval vegetable is not as common as once thought either.

From a distance, it is difficult to tell the Madrid and Normandie pitchers apart. I once made a hundred yard dash in no time flat for a pink "Madrid" larger pitcher only to discover it was pink Normandie. When I saw the five dollar price, I felt a little better, but not nearly so well as I would have felt had that been a Madrid pitcher in that shape.

I would still like to see a piece in green; but so far none has turned up so I will continue to omit it.

	AMBER	PINK	IRIDES-CENT
Bowl, 5" Berry	1.50	1.50	1.50
*Bowl, 6½" Cereal	2.00	2.50	2.25
Bowl, 8½" Large Berry	4.50	6.00	4.75
Bowl, 10" Oval Veg.	5.50	10.00	6.00
Creamer, Footed	2.50	3.00	3.00
Cup	2.00	2.25	2.50
Pitcher, 8", 80 oz.	25.00	40.00	
Plate, 6" Sherbet	1.25	1.25	1.50
Plate, 8" Salad	2.00	2.50	2.50
Plate, 9¼" Luncheon	2.50	3.00	3.00
Plate, 11" Dinner	3.25	7.00	3.50
Plate, 11" Grill	2.50	4.50	3.00

	AMBER	PINK	IRIDES-CENT
Platter, 11¾"	5.50	7.75	6.00
Salt and Pepper, Pr.	20.00	27.50	
Saucer	1.50	1.50	1.50
Sherbet	2.00	3.00	2.50
Sugar	2.50	2.50	3.00
Sugar Lid	40.00	65.00	
Tumbler, 4", 5 oz.			
Juice	5.00	8.00	
Tumbler, 4¼", 9 oz.			
Water	6.00	9.00	
Tumbler, 5", 12 oz.			
Iced Tea	8.00	12.00	

*Mistaken by many as butter bottom.

Please refer to Foreword for pricing information

NO. 610, "PYRAMID"

(green, pink, yellow, crystal)   (Black, 1974-75 by Tiara)

INDIANA GLASS COMPANY
1928-1932

This simplistic yet stately pattern is reminiscent of Tearoom in general shape and weight of glass. The four part relish, in fact, is often mistaken for Tearoom by novice collectors. Yet, the same collectors who simply can't abide Tearoom, will like this pattern. What's your opinion?

Crystal, yellow and pink pitchers, respectively, are hard to find. The green is more frequently seen. Tumblers, available in both 8 and 11 ounce size, are rarely seen in any color in the 11 ounce size.

Latch on to any ice buckets you find, particularly if they have the lid. I also looked for the 9½ inch oval vegetable and the 9½ inch handled pickle dish in all my wanderings and was unable to come up with either; that should clue you to their availability.

The creamer and sugar came with or without the stand shown; these and the berry set are the most often seen pieces.
Keep in mind that the black items you will see in this pattern were made in 1974 and 1975 for Tiara.

	CRYSTAL/PINK	GREEN	YELLOW
Bowl, 4¾" Berry	2.50	2.50	4.00
Bowl, 8½" Master Berry	7.50	8.00	12.00
Bowl, 9½" Oval	15.00	15.00	20.00
Bowl, 9½" Pickle	15.00	15.00	20.00
Creamer	5.00	5.00	7.50
Ice Tub	15.00	15.00	20.00
Ice Tub and Lid	30.00	30.00	40.00
Pitcher	60.00	45.00	100.00
Relish Tray, 4 Part, Handled	10.00	10.00	14.00
Tray for Creamer and Sugar	7.50	7.50	10.00
Tumbler, 8 ounce, Footed	6.00	6.00	8.50
Tumbler, 11 ounce, Footed	12.50	15.00	17.50

125

NO. 612, "HORSESHOE"

(green, yellow, pink, crystal)

INDIANA GLASS COMPANY

1930-1933

Horseshoe is another of Indiana's numbered patterns that was named by collectors. I had started to say "aptly named" until I took a second look at the "Horseshoe" and then I reneged. Perhaps those people's horses wore fancier shoes than I'm accustomed to seeing; or maybe these are "Sunday" horseshoes!

Newcomers should know that plates come with or without the center motif. Grill plates in this pattern are very rarely seen; it is fortunate that not every collector wants them.

A discovery in the sizes of bowls has been made which may affect some collectors. Indiana listed bowls at 7½ and 9 inches. They are found in 7½, 8½, and 9½ inches. This may cause some collectors to be in search of another size bowl.

Notice that crystal sugar bowl which adds yet another color to our list.

The bottom of the pink candy dish is not the one usually found. You can see the more commonly found one in the green. Only the lid has the pattern on candy dishes.

Tall, footed iced tea glasses have long since become scarce; so, if you haven't gotten them by now, when you do find them, you may need a private gold mine.

It will take time to know for certain, but for now the 9 ounce flat tumbler is much more plentiful than the 12 ounce flat tumbler. The one shown in the first two editions was bought cheaply because no one knew what the pattern was at the time; it's been a long time since any one has repeated that mistake.

Horseshoe items have generally followed the upward trend in price that most Depression Glass patterns have made; however, the yellow pitcher has dropped a bit in price due to so many showing up as compared to what was previously known. I have never seen a grill plate or a butter dish in yellow although one of the latter supposedly sold at auction only thirty miles from Lexington. I could never confirm this, however.

	GREEN	YELLOW
Bowl, 4½" Berry	7.00	8.00
Bowl, 6½" Cereal	7.00	8.00
Bowl, 7½" Salad	6.00	8.00
Bowl, 8½" Vegetable	9.00	10.00
Bowl, 9½" Large Berry	9.50	11.00
Bowl, 10½" Oval Vegetable	6.75	7.75
Butter Dish and Cover	400.00	*
Candy in Metal Holder		
Motif on Lid —		
Also, Pink— ($100.00)	90.00	
Creamer, Footed	4.75	5.00
Cup	3.00	3.25
Pitcher, 8½, 64 oz.	157.50	167.50
Plate, 6" Sherbet	1.50	1.50

	GREEN	YELLOW
Plate, 8⅜" Salad	2.25	2.25
Plate, 9⅜" Luncheon	2.50	2.50
Plate, 10⅜" Dinner	3.25	3.50
Plate, 10⅜" Grill	8.00	8.00
Plate, 11¼" Sandwich	5.50	6.00
Platter, 10¾" Oval	7.00	7.75
Relish, 3 Part, Footed	5.00	6.00
Saucer	2.50	3.00
Sherbet	6.00	7.00
Sugar, Open	4.75	5.00
Tumbler, 4¼", 9 oz.	42.50	
Tumbler, 4¾", 12 oz	65.00	
Tumbler, 9 oz., Footed	6.75	7.75
Tumbler, 12 oz., Footed	40.00	50.00

*Have never seen one but have had reports of them.

127

NO. 616, "VERNON"

(green, crystal, yellow)

INDIANA GLASS COMPANY
1930-1932

From this picture, there is no where else to go with this pattern. All pieces that are known to exist in Number 616 are shown.

The tumblers are not very durable as we broke two in a little over a month's usage before I retired them. (My wife still believes that everything should be usable; I just couldn't stand the strain.) You can break a raft of "Big Top" or "Welch's" glasses before they cost as much as two of these tumblers. We finally completed four place settings of each color with the exception of green tumblers. For a while I couldn't find any in yellow, but they turned up; so I have hope yet for the green!

You will have "a time" finding any of this pattern as it just isn't that plentiful. The green seems more difficult than the rest to ferret out. I enjoy the crystal trimmed with a platinum band, but then, I've got those tumblers to enjoy.

It's an intriguingly designed pattern and it's a shame there are so few pieces to be had. A four place setting only has nineteen pieces unless you want more than one sandwich plate.

	GREEN	CRYSTAL	YELLOW
Creamer, Footed	17.50	8.00	15.00
Cup	12.50	5.00	9.50
Plate, 8" Luncheon	8.00	5.00	7.00
Plate, 11" Sandwich	20.00	12.00	18.00
Saucer	5.00	3.00	4.00
Sugar, Footed	17.50	7.00	15.00
Tumbler, 5", Footed	22.50	10.00	15.00

Please refer to Foreword for pricing information

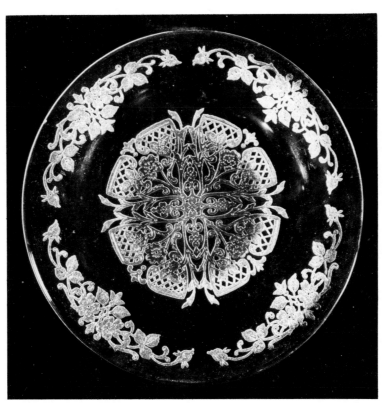

129

NO. 618, "PINEAPPLE & FLORAL"

(crystal, amber, red)

INDIANA GLASS COMPANY
1932-1937

The green Pineapple and Floral plate shown still hasn't found any neighbors even though the man who sold it to me assured me he'd had other pieces in green. It's certainly been well hidden so far. Who has it?

A few more of the fired on red pieces have surfaced though none different from those pictured.

A reader wrote about my guess concerning the usage of the big flower vase shown lying on its side. She sent word that they still use two of these in metal floor stands in their funeral home for flowers. So my "attached to the wall via a wire base and holding flowers" was not so far wrong!

The only diamond shaped comport it is safe to buy as "old" is the fired on red or the amber. You can get this comport, today, in crystal and sundry other colors at your local glass barn for 59¢ - 79¢.

There are three sizes of tumblers; but none are easily found. A large portion of those that are found have mold roughness so bad around the top that you can cut your mouth trying to drink from them! My wife had me collect a set of these for her to use, but when she felt the roughness of the tumblers, she gave it all back. If you can't use it, she doesn't want it!

Sherbet and cream soups will not jump out at you. You will really have to "beat the bushes" for them.

	CRYSTAL	AMBER/ RED
Ash Tray, 4½"	4.00	4.50
Bowl, 6" Cereal	1.50	2.00
Bowl, 7" Salad	4.00	5.00
Bowl, 10" Oval Vegetable	4.25	5.00
Comport, Diamond Shaped	.50	3.00
Creamer,		
Diamond Shaped	3.00	5.00
Cream Soup	7.50	10.00
Cup	3.50	4.00
Plate, 6" Sherbet	1.50	2.00
Plate, 8⅜" Salad	2.25	3.50
*Plate, 9⅜" Dinner	3.25	4.00
Plate, 10½" Grill	2.25	3.00

*Green — $10.00

	CRYSTAL	AMBER/ RED
Plate, 11½" Sandwich	4.50	6.00
Platter, 11" Closed Handles	5.00	5.75
Platter, Relish, 11½", Divided	4.00	4.50
Saucer	1.50	2.00
Sherbet, Footed	4.00	4.50
Sugar, Diamond Shaped	3.00	5.00
Tidbit, 2 Tier		
8⅜" and 11½" Plates	10.00	12.50
Tidbit, 2 Tier		
6" and 9⅜" Plates	8.00	10.00
Tumbler, 4", 9 oz.	10.00	12.00
Tumbler, 4¼", 10½" oz.	10.00	12.00
Tumbler, 4½", 12 oz.	12.00	12.00
Vase, Cone Shaped	15.00	
Vase Holder ($15.00)		

131

OLD CAFE

(pink, crystal, ruby red)

HOCKING GLASS COMPANY
1936-1938; 1940

Trying to collect a set of Old Cafe in the basic pieces is a chore, or would be if anyone did it. Mostly the occasional pieces in this are collected to "fill the gaps" in other similar patterns. The pattern is geometrically shaped and looks nice on a table; but there are very few collectors of the pattern per se.

A 7¼ inch vase has shown up that wasn't hitherto known; but even the fellow dealer who pointed it out to me was not exactly jumping for joy over its discovery. Maybe he was just naturally blase? You can't even find this vase turned upside down and drilled through to make a lamp. One reader has a pair of these in Royal Ruby.

Hocking reissued a few pieces of this during their Royal Ruby promotion of 1940 and these few pieces of red do more changing of hands than does any of the rest of this pattern put together.

I'm making this sound worse than it is. The pattern itself is nice enough. It's just that there are so few basic pieces around to be "discovered" that the pattern hasn't had a chance to catch on with collectors. If your grandmother handed you down a complete setting of it, don't throw it out! You can, in fact, be quite proud of it as, again, it does look very nice in a table setting.

	CRYSTAL, PINK	ROYAL RUBY		CRYSTAL, PINK	ROYAL RUBY
Bowl, 3¾" Berry	.75	3.00	Plate, 6" Sherbet	.75	
Bowl, 5", One or Two Handles	1.25		Plate, 10" Dinner	2.00	
			Salt and Pepper, Pr.	*	
Bowl, 5½" Cereal	1.25		Saucer	.75	
Bowl, 9", Closed Handles	3.00	8.00	Sherbet, Low Footed	1.25	
Candy Dish, 8" Low	2.50	6.00	Tumbler, 3" Juice	1.50	
Cup	1.50	3.00	Tumbler, 4" Water	2.00	
Lamp		12.50	Vase, 7¼"	6.00	10.00
Olive Dish, 6" Oblong	1.50				

*Item should exist as listed in old
catalogs and publications but can
not be confirmed by author.

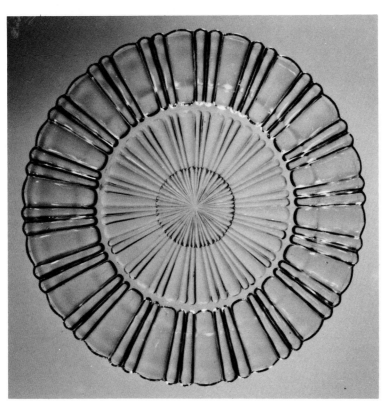

133

OLD ENGLISH, "THREADING"

(green, pink, amber)

INDIANA GLASS COMPANY

Late 1920's

Welcome to the world of amber Old English which has never been shown before!

Several new items have shown themselves and there are bound to be more. A sherbet was found in Lancaster, Ohio, the home of Hocking? A cheese and cracker set, consisting of a 3½ inch comport on an indented plate (similar to the one in Flower Garden and Butterfly) and an eight inch serving bowl have journeyed from the dark unknown into the light of discovery. You can see the indented plate in the pattern shot as it was found after the big photo was taken.

I saw another piece which appeared to be a type of vase in an antique shop in southern Kentucky. Unfortunately, as often happens when you're passing by, the shop was closed on that particular day and my through-the-window gazing can't be considered too accurate. I left a note and stamp to write me about the price or at least to send the measurements of the vase which I thought was sage; but I never saw said stamp again.

The candy lid that graces the foreground is in need of a bottom. I first thought this to be the pitcher lid; but, alas, it was too small. My amber pitcher could use a lid, or perhaps your top needs a pitcher?

	PINK, GREEN AMBER
Bowl, 9" Footed Fruit	12.00
Bowl, 9½" Flat	12.00
Candlesticks, 4", Pr.	12.50
Candy Jar with Lid	15.00
Compote, 3½" Tall, 7" Across	7.00
Creamer	6.50
Fruit Stand, 11" Footed	12.00
Pitcher and Cover	47.50
Plate, Indent for Compote	10.00
Sandwich Server, Center Handle	8.50
Sherbet	6.00
Sugar	6.50
Sugar Cover	6.50
Tumbler, 4½" Footed	5.50
Tumbler, 5½" Footed	7.00
Vase, 13"	15.00

Please refer to Foreword for pricing information

135

OVIDE, incorrectly dubbed "New Century"

(green, white, black)

HAZEL ATLAS GLASS COMPANY
1930-1935

The "Art Deco" set in Ovide caught the eye of several people when the book first came out and I had a couple of reports of other sets; but I have not been able to confirm them.

The discovery of an 11 inch platter in platonite hardly stirred the Depression people; but it is described as having black and red trim as does the plate shown in the background. Platonite, should you not know, was a specially made, heat resistant ware that was marketed by the Hazel Atlas Company. It was more expensive generally; but it normally came with fired-on colors like the yellow cup and saucer pictured. The reason the black and red trimmed pieces are so unstimulating is because they look like restaurant dishes which are hardly exciting unless you're dining in an ultra posh place.

The futuristic oviform which is typical of the pieces is clearly represented by the green sugar and creamer pictured.

	GREEN	BLACK/ DECORATED WHITE		GREEN	BLACK/ DECORATED WHITE
Bowl, 4¾" Berry	1.00	5.00	Plate, 6" Sherbet	.75	1.50
Bowl, 5½" Cereal	1.25	5.50	Plate, 8" Luncheon	1.25	3.25
Bowl, 8" Large Berry	2.25	12.50	Plate, 9" Dinner		4.50
Candy Dish and Cover	10.00	17.50	Platter, 11"		6.00
Cocktail, Fruit, Footed	1.00	4.00	Salt and Pepper, Pr.	5.50	12.00
Creamer	2.00	5.50	Saucer	.75	1.50
Cup	1.00	2.50	Sherbet	1.00	4.00
			Sugar, Open	2.00	5.50

OYSTER AND PEARL

(pink, crystal, ruby red, white with fired on pink or green)

ANCHOR HOCKING GLASS
1938-1940

Oyster and Pearl candleholders are the most commonly found pieces of this pattern which was first made in crystal and pink in 1938. In 1940 during Anchor Hocking's promotion of the Royal Ruby, pieces were made in red. It's generally pieces of the latter color which are more in demand today.

Ever since I placed my 170 pounds right in the middle of the 13½ inch pink sandwich plate on my return from photographing the first book, I've had a hard time convincing myself to buy this pattern; but I finally bought the complete set in Royal Ruby after this picture was taken. And they make spectacular center piece items! The large bowls are great for keeping fruit, and frankly, it's hard to buy a large modern bowl that isn't plastic or that would be as attractive for the price.

The pink and white fired on pieces went by the name "Dusty Rose" and the green and white were called "Spring Green". They are not very popular today nor were they when they were issued.

	CRYSTAL, PINK	ROYAL RUBY	WHITE WITH FIRED ON GREEN OR PINK
Bowl, 5¼" Round or Handled	1.75	5.00	3.00
Bowl, 5¼" Heart Shaped, One Handled	2.50	6.50	3.00
Bowl, 6½" Deep, Handled	3.00	5.50	
Bowl, 10½" Fruit, Deep	5.00	15.00	8.00
Candleholder, 3½", Pr.	5.00	17.50	9.00
Plate, 13½" Sandwich	4.50	13.50	
Relish Dish, 10¼" Oblong	3.00	6.00	4.00

Please refer to Foreword for pricing information

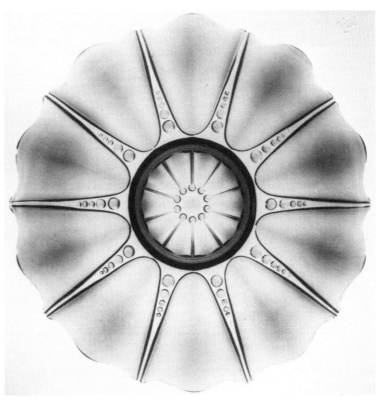

139

"PARROT", SYLVAN

(green, amber, crystal)

FEDERAL GLASS COMPANY
1931-1932

The real name of this pattern, Sylvan, would draw some blank stares were you to ask dealers for it. Everyone calls it "Parrot" which makes a great deal more sense since you see more of the birds than you do of the "wooded area".

Hardly worth mentioning to veteran collectors is the fact that a supply of thirty or so green pitchers found in an old closed hardware store has been totally absorbed by the market. Until that "find", it was thought there weren't any green Parrot pitchers to be had. Now, people who missed getting one of those are wishing for another such cache!

The amber color is being just as eagerly sought by collectors as the green though the supply of it, never very good, seems to have about dried up.

Amber platters and tumblers are all more difficult to locate than the green; but until an amber pitcher surfaces, the tumblers shouldn't raise much more in price. Except for the odd heavy footed tumbler at the rear of the picture, all tumblers are thin and are reminiscent of Madrid in shape.

Amber shakers in Parrot have still not shown themselves; and only two butter dishes in amber are complete so far though there are various separate butter tops and bottoms in the hands of collectors who are hoping for the other piece. I number in this last group as I still need the top.

An amber covered sugar and creamer are not shown for the simple fact that after I had already purchased them from a dealer, she resold them to someone else! A friend of mine refers to this as putting a price tag on your integrity; I just avoid ever doing business again with such persons no matter what they have.

Keep in mind that the amber grill plates are square while the grill plates in green are round. Know, too, that the thin, round luncheon plates you find with parrots and flowers in the design were made by Indiana Glass Company and are not part of this set.

Butter dish tops and sugar tops IN MINT CONDITION are hard to find. There are plenty around with chips and damaged places. Look for damage to the easily chipped points sticking out on the cups before you buy. All prices quoted in this book are for mint condition pieces.

	GREEN	AMBER
Bowl, 5" Berry	4.50	4.25
Bowl, 7" Soup	7.00	7.00
Bowl, 8" Large Berry	22.50	25.00
Bowl, 10" Oval Vegetable	10.00	12.50
Butter Dish and Cover	150.00	325.00
Creamer, Footed	7.50	8.00
Cup	6.75	7.50
Hot Plate, 5"	125.00	
Pitcher, 8½', 80 oz.	275.00	
Plate, 5¾" Sherbet	3.00	3.50
Plate, 7½" Salad	4.50	
Plate, 9" Dinner	6.50	7.00
Plate, 10½" Grill, Round	5.50	
Plate, 10½" Grill, Square		5.50

	GREEN	AMBER
Plate, 10¼" Square	8.50	8.50
Platter, 11¼" Oblong	10.00	25.00
Salt and Pepper, Pr.	97.50	
Saucer	3.00	3.00
Sherbet, Footed, Cone	6.00	7.00
Sherbet, 4¼" High	40.00	
Sugar	7.50	8.00
Sugar Cover	20.00	30.00
Tumbler, 4¼", 10 oz.	35.00	40.00
Tumbler, 5½", 12 oz.	37.50	42.50
Tumbler, 5¾" Footed, Heavy	35.00	40.00
Tumbler, 5½", 10 oz. Thin (Madrid Mold)		50.00

141

PATRICIAN, "SPOKE"

(pink, green, amber, crystal)

FEDERAL GLASS COMPANY

1933-37

Borders were important to the Roman nobleman. The purple border of his elaborately draped toga set him apart from people of lesser rank. His buildings and tombs were intricately and beautifully bordered. Whoever designed this pattern for Federal picked up several of the more elaborate border designs thought up by ancient artisans and placed them around the outside edge of this pattern. In the middle he drew the wheel of a racing chariot; and thus he made the pattern we call Patrician. The "plebians" on this side of the Atlantic dubbed it "Spoke" from the center motif which probably reminded them more of wagon or buggy wheels than of racing chariot's.

Collectors who turned to pink have been stymied at finding the pitcher, butter dish or shakers. I was hopeful of making them sit up and take notice of a pink cookie jar in the photo; but it didn't work out. One was supposedly shipped to someone in New York; so, if you've got it, I'd certainly appreciate a confirming snap shot. The elusive green one is pictured.

Sugar lids IN MINT CONDITION are another problem to find, particularly in crystal. The pink one is just more in demand and, thus, the price differential.

The supply of once plentiful amber Patrician is slowly dwindling with only the dinner plates remaining easy to get. Whoever promoted the plates in the 1930's certainly excelled at his work. I've seen them everywhere I've traveled. My Dad won a set as a child for selling the most newspapers. How did your family get them?

In the past, I have listed three sizes of pitchers. However, since only two sizes have been located, I'm only going to list those two. Please notice that there are different types of handles on the pitchers. The pitcher with a molded handle, shown in both green and pink, holds 75 ounces and is 8 inches tall; the pitcher with an applied handle, shown in crystal, holds 75 ounces and is 8¼ inches tall. I simply can't find a pitcher that holds 60 or 68 ounces.

There are variations in the sizes of tumblers, also; so I have listed what I have found and not what the old catalogue listings have since they simply don't "tell it like it is". There are three flat tumblers: 4 inch, 5 ounce; 4½ inch, 9 ounce; and 5½ inch, 14 ounce. The footed tumbler is 5¼ inches tall and holds 8 ounces. Should you have sizes other than these, I would appreciate hearing from you.

	AMBER, CRYSTAL	PINK	GREEN
Bowl, 4¾", Cream Soup	3.50	10.00	7.00
Bowl, 5" Berry	1.75	6.50	2.50
Bowl, 6" Cereal	3.00	6.00	3.50
Bowl, 8½" Large Berry	5.50	8.50	8.00
Bowl, 12" Oval Vegetable	5.00	8.00	6.00
Butter Dish and Cover	40.00	175.00	60.00
Cookie Jar and Cover	25.00		100.00
Creamer, Footed	2.75	3.50	2.75
Cup	2.00	3.00	2.25
Pitcher, 8", 75 oz.	30.00	75.00	65.00
Pitcher, 8¼", 75 oz.	30.00	80.00	70.00
Plate, 6" Sherbet	1.25	1.50	1.25
Plate, 7½" Salad	4.50	9.00	5.00

	AMBER, CRYSTAL	PINK	GREEN
Plate, 9" Luncheon	2.00	3.50	3.50
Plate, 10½" Dinner	2.50	9.00	7.50
Plate, 10½" Grill	4.00	6.00	6.00
Platter, 11½" Oval	4.75	7.50	7.50
Salt and Pepper, Pr.	22.00	45.00	27.50
Saucer	1.00	1.50	1.25
Sherbet	3.00	6.00	6.00
Sugar	2.75	3.50	2.75
Sugar Cover	8.00	30.00	25.00
Tumbler, 4", 5 oz.	8.50	10.00	7.75
Tumbler, 4½", 9 oz.	8.50	10.00	6.00
Tumbler, 5½", 14 oz.	10.00	17.50	12.00
Tumbler, 5¼", 8 oz. Footed	12.00		15.00

143

PEAR OPTIC, "THUMBPRINT"

(green)

FEDERAL GLASS COMPANY

1929-30

Pear Optic is often confused with "Raindrops"; so flip to that pattern now and notice that those "raindrops" are round impressions and not the longated "thumbprint" ones of Pear Optic.

You may possibly find a quantity of this somewhere, but I wasn't that lucky and had a devil of a time trying to round up pieces for the photograph. The sherbet came from a shop in St. Petersburg, Florida, where you had to first wipe the piece in order to see what pattern lay beneath the grime and where you could get wet in a rain storm standing under the "roof".

This is one of the less expensive patterns to collect which has the added bonus of having a good assortment of pieces available; it's also a colored glassware. Most of the less expensive glassware is found in crystal.

	GREEN		GREEN
Bowl, 4¾" Berry	1.25	Salt and Pepper, Pr.	8.75
Bowl, 5" Cereal	1.50	Saucer	.50
Bowl, 8" Large Berry	3.50	Sherbet	1.50
Creamer, Footed	1.75	Sugar, Footed	1.75
Cup	1.50	Tumbler, 4", 5 oz.	2.00
Plate, 6" Sherbet	.75	Tumbler, 5", 10 oz.	2.50
Plate, 8" Luncheon	1.50	Tumbler, 5½", 12 oz.	3.00
Plate, 9¼" Dinner	2.00	Whiskey, 2¼", 1 oz.	3.00

145

PETALWARE

(pink, crystal, monax, cremax, cobalt and fired on yellow, blue, green & red)

MACBETH EVANS GLASS COMPANY

1930-40

After looking at the black and white picture of Petalware in the last two books, I hope you appreciate the color.

You often find plates in Petalware with paintings of flowers or fruits and made to hang on the wall for decoration. I saw a set of eight different paintings at a garage sale here; but since they were only $12.50 each, I allowed them to remain with those people who obviously treasured them more than I.

The newest listing for this pattern is a saucer for the cream soup. The indentation is too large for the cup, but it just fits the cream soup bottom.

There are no salt and pepper shakers for Petalware per se; however, as mentioned before, the monax shakers in Newport will serve here.

The pieces pictured at the right of the photograph are in the cremax or clam-like color.

The remaining white pieces are in the monax color.

The fired-on blue cup was part of a set. You will find fired-on yellow, green and red pieces also.

Several pieces are showing up in cobalt blue, namely the 9 inch bowl, sherbet and creamer and sugar. The first two items I've seen personally; a friend saw the creamer and sugar sell at $15.00 each and was certain they were "true blue" and not a fired-on blue.

Left out of the last book by oversight was the commonly found cobalt blue mustard on an attached plate having a metal top.

I bought a hanging chandelier having one large Petalware shade and five smaller ones intending that you see it; but there just seemed no way to show it adequately.

	PINK, CRYSTAL	CREMAX, MONAX Plain	Fired-On Decorations
Bowl, 4½" Cream Soup	2.50	3.50	5.00
Bowl, 5¾" Cereal	1.75	2.50	4.00
*Bowl, 8¾" Large Berry	3.50	6.00	8.50
Cup	1.75	2.50	3.00
**Creamer, Footed	2.25	3.00	4.00
Lamp Shade (Many Sizes) $3.00 to $6.00			
Mustard with Metal Cover in Cobalt Blue Only $3.50			
Pitcher, 80 oz.	15.00		
Plate, 6" Sherbet	1.00	1.75	2.25

*Also in cobalt at 27.50
**Also in cobalt at 15.00

	PINK, CRYSTAL	CREMAX, MONAX Plain	Fired-On Decorations
Plate, 8" Salad	1.50	2.50	3.00
Plate, 9" Dinner	2.00	3.00	4.00
Plate, 11" Salver	3.00	4.50	6.00
Plate, 12" Salver		6.00	8.00
Platter, 13" Oval	5.00	7.00	8.00
Saucer	1.00	1.25	1.50
**Sherbet, Low Footed	1.50	2.75	4.00
**Sugar, Footed	2.25	3.00	4.00
Tidbit Servers or Lazy Susans several styles 10.00 to 15.00			
***Tumblers (Crystal Decorated Bands) 3.00 to 6.00			

*** Several Sizes

147

PRINCESS

(green, 2 yellows, pink, blue)

HOCKING GLASS COMPANY
1931-35

There are at least four of those sinful blue cookie jars in Princess now. I say "sinful" because they cause one to covet! I've seen all but one of them and they are beautiful! None quite have the lurid background that the first one that was stolen has, but the proud owners could care less. The one shown is not the one pictured on the cover of the last book; another sold in Ohio; and another went from Virginia to Georgia. Doesn't it excite you to know they're lurking out there, somewhere?

Prices for green Princess have soared lately with an increase in demand for it and with the pieces getting harder and harder to find. This is particularly true of the candy dish and the tall, footed iced tea glasses.

Several green pitchers have shown up "footed" like the one shown on last year's cover; however, these latter ones all have frosted panels down the design. There are tumblers with this same frosting business to go with the pitchers. Frankly, this is one place where I, personally, prefer "last year's model".

Collectors of yellow Princess will please note the two colors photographed! At left is the honey amber or "apricot" yellow; on the right is the topaz yellow.

The price for yellow shakers jumped.

To date, no yellow lid to the yellow Princess butter bottom has been found.

One of the few pink ash trays that surfaced is pictured in the front.

	GREEN	PINK	YELLOW AMBER
Ash Tray, 4½"	15.00	20.00	20.00
Bowl, 4½" Berry	4.00	4.00	5.00
Bowl, 5" Cereal or Oatmeal	5.00	5.00	6.00
Bowl, 9" Salad, Octagonal	9.50	8.00	15.00
Bowl, 9½" Hat Shaped	12.00	9.00	15.00
Bowl, 10" Oval Vegetable	8.00	7.00	15.00
Butter Dish and Cover	45.00	52.50	250.00
Cake Stand, 10"	6.00	6.50	*
Candy Dish and Cover	20.00	15.00	*
Coaster	12.00	10.00	20.00
†Cookie Jar and Cover	15.00	12.00	*
Creamer, Oval	3.00	2.50	4.50
††Cup	3.00	2.50	3.00
Pitcher, 6", 37 oz.	12.50	10.00	50.00
Pitcher, 7⅜", 24 oz. Footed	250.00		
Pitcher, 8", 60 oz.	20.00	17.50	37.50
Plate, 5½", Sherbet	1.50	1.00	1.50
Plate, 8" Salad	3.50	2.00	4.00
Plate, 9½" Dinner	4.00	3.00	5.00
††Plate, 9½ Grill	3.50	2.50	3.50

	GREEN	PINK	YELLOW AMBER
Plate, 10½", Grill, Closed Handles	3.00	3.00	4.00
Plate, 11½", Sandwich, Handled	5.00	5.00	5.00
Platter, 12" Closed Handles	7.50	6.00	8.50
Relish, 7½", Divided or Plain	7.00	6.00	9.00
Salt and Pepper, Pr., 4½"	22.50	17.00	35.00
Spice Shakers, Pr. 5½"	15.00	*	
Saucer (Same as Sherbet Plate)	1.50	1.00	1.50
Sherbet, Footed	4.00	3.00	7.00
Sugar	3.00	2.50	4.50
Sugar Cover	3.00	2.50	4.50
Tidbit, Two Tier	45.00		
Tumbler, 3", 5 oz. Juice	9.00	5.50	9.00
Tumbler, 4", 9 oz. Water	8.00	5.50	6.50
Tumbler, 5¼", 12 oz. Iced Tea	12.00	8.00	12.00
Tumbler, 4¾", 9 oz. Sq. Ft.	30.00		
Tumbler, 5¼", 10 oz. Footed	9.00	6.00	8.50
Tumbler, 6½", Footed, 12½ oz.	17.00	15.00	*
Vase, 8"	12.00	12.00	*

Please refer to Foreword for pricing information

†Blue — 300.00
††Blue — 35.00

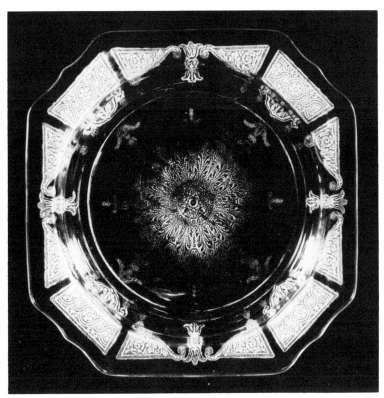

149

QUEEN MARY, "VERTICAL RIBBED"

(pink, crystal)

HOCKING GLASS COMPANY
1936-40

Before warning you that they were hard to find, I believe I should have bought a few of those Queen Mary butter dishes or "preserve dishes" as they were listed. From $12 to $65 is quite a jump. A few have sold for more, I've been told; but they can be bought for the price listed.

Queen Mary shakers came with both metal and plastic tops; so don't worry if you find them with red plastic tops.

This pattern is plentiful enough to be collectible in crystal for beginners. The prices on the pink may be prohibitive to persons on a limited budget. For instance, pink dinner plates will cost you about $6.00 each while crystal dinner plates run about $2.00 each. If you were collecting for an eight or twelve piece place setting, the difference on dinner plates alone would buy you many accessory pieces in crystal.

Pink shakers and a pink candy dish may be a little hard to find; but they shouldn't reach the price of the butter dish; so let's not go overboard just because I said they were a bit hard to find!

	PINK, CRYSTAL
Ash Tray, Oval, 2" x 3¾"	1.25
Bowl, 4", One Handle or None	1.00
Bowls, 5" Berry, 6" Cereal	1.25
Bowl, 5½", Two Handles	1.00
Bowl, 8¾" Large Berry	2.50
*Butter Dish or Preserve and Cover	15.00
Candy Dish and Cover	10.00
Candlesticks, 4½", Double Branch, Pr.	5.50
Candlesticks, Ruby Red, Pr.	14.00
Celery or Pickle Dish, 5" x 10"	1.25
Cigarette Jar, Oval, 2" x 3"	2.00
Coaster, 3½"	1.00
Coaster/Ash Tray, 4¼" Square	3.00
Comport, 5¾"	2.50
Creamer, Oval	2.00

	PINK, CRYSTAL
Cup	2.00
Plate, 6" and 6⅝"	1.50
Plate, 8½" Salad	3.00
**Plate, 9¾" Dinner	4.50
Plate, 12" Sandwich	3.00
Plate, 14" Serving Tray	4.00
Relish Tray, 12", 3 Part	3.00
Relish Tray, 14", 4 Part	3.50
***Salt and Pepper, Pr.	9.00
Saucer	.50
Sherbet, Footed	1.75
Sugar, Oval	2.00
Tumbler, 3½", 5 oz. Juice	1.00
Tumbler, 4", 9 oz. Water	1.50
Tumbler, 5", 10 oz. Footed	2.00

*Pink — 65.00
**Pink — 6.00
***Pink — 20.00

RAINDROPS, "OPTIC DESIGN"

(green, crystal)

FEDERAL GLASS COMPANY
1929-33

Allow me to introduce you to Mr. Raindrop Saltshaker. He's been with us nearly two years, now, and he's been looking that whole time for a "Mrs.". See what you can do.

The rounded, bump-like impressions are inside the shaker. Again, the impressions are ROUND and not elongated as are those of Pear Optic. Pear Optic impressions are "scooped out" in the middle, too, while Raindrops impressions are little hills or raised bumps appearing on the inside of pieces or on the underside as with plates.

That crystal tumbler almost got lost on the white background; but if you strain your eyes, you can see it between the two green tumblers.

The sugar lid still rates as one of Depression Glass's rarest; however, since this pattern is not highly collected, the price has not streaked into the beyond via rockets. I have seen sixteen Mayfair lids, for example; I have only seen two in Raindrops. However, to date, the two patterns are equal in having only one footed shaker turn up in Mayfair and only one shaker in Raindrops to turn up at all.

The sherbet and sherbet plate have never crossed my line of vision; I'm beginning to wonder if they really do exist.

The little 4½ inch bowl is a new discovery.

If you never have, get out and visit some antique shops and flea markets. Maybe you'll be the one to find something really rare. At any rate, I'll bet you have fun!

	GREEN
Bowl, 4½" Fruit	1.00
Bowl, 6" Cereal	1.25
Cup	2.00
Creamer	1.50
Plate, 6" Sherbet	.75
Plate, 8" Luncheon	1.25

	GREEN
Salt and Pepper, Pr.	20.00
Saucer	1.00
Sherbet	1.50
Sugar	1.50
Sugar Cover	15.00
Tumbler, 3", 4 oz.	2.50
Whiskey, 1⅞"	3.00

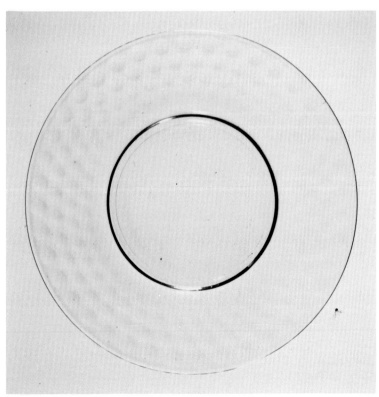

153

RIBBON

(green, black, crystal)

HAZEL ATLAS GLASS COMPANY

1930-32

Notice that Ribbon pieces are of similar shape to pieces of Cloverleaf and Ovide. Molds were terribly expensive, but they could be re-designed as far as pattern; so Hazel Atlas was just getting its money's worth, so to speak. This was commonly practiced by glass companies.

You will find shakers in both crystal and pink. Although I have not seen the pink myself, a collector of shakers says she has them in pink.

Few pieces are showing up in black; but shakers, bowl, and creamer and sugar are possible as they have all been seen. One of the items still hoped for in black is the candy dish.

The green candy dish has raised a bit in price.

	GREEN	BLACK		GREEN	BLACK
Bowl, 4" Berry	1.00		Salt and Pepper, Pr.	9.00	17.50
Bowl, 8" Large Berry	4.00	12.00	Saucer	1.00	
Candy Dish and Cover	17.50		Sherbet, Footed	1.75	
Creamer, Footed	2.00	7.50	Sugar, Footed	2.00	7.50
Cup	1.50		Tumbler, 4", 9 oz.	3.00	
Plate, 6¼" Sherbet	1.00		Tumbler, 5½", 10 oz.	4.50	
Plate, 8" Luncheon	1.75	7.00	Tumbler, 6½", 13 oz.	4.50	

Please refer to Foreword for pricing information

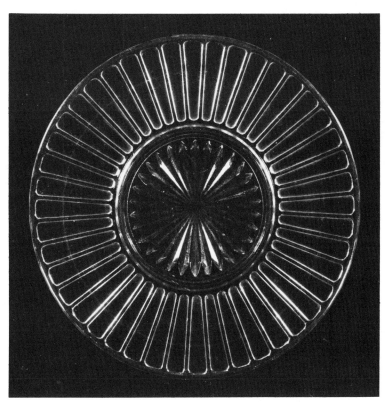

155

RING, "BANDED RINGS"

(crystal, green and crystal w/decoration, pink, red, blue)

HOCKING GLASS COMPANY

1927-32

The pattern shot for Ring was made of a beautiful shade of blue very similar to the Mayfair blue; unfortunately, due to some of said shots being very off-color, they were scrapped in favor of black and white.

You are viewing the red plate I talked about last time. See, I told you it was pretty!

As I've indicated before, a gigantic headache is possible trying to match the colored stripes on this pattern. Notice the color combinations here: yellow, orange; yellow, orange, green; yellow, red, black; yellow, red, orange, black; yes, there are other combinations as well. The crystal with a platinum band is especially sought by some.

Notice the two styles of pitchers as well as the decanter and cocktail shaker. That green shaker shown is very rarely found. So memorize it.

The crystal is by far the easiest to obtain with the pastel decorated and the green being next hardest. The pink only occurs in pitcher and tumblers. The most difficult, of course, are the unusual colors of blue and red which were either specially ordered items or experimental pieces. So far, these unusual colors have only been found in an 8 inch luncheon plate.

For the initiate collector, this pattern offers ease of collection, variety of pieces, variety of color combinations, and best of all, it's still reasonably priced for glass that is one of Depression's oldest patterns. Not everyone even recognizes this as Depression Glass, so you can perhaps even find it at prices less than those quoted here on occasion.

	CRYSTAL	CRYSTAL DECOR. GREEN
Bowl, 5" Berry	.50	1.00
Bowl, 8" Large Berry	2.00	3.00
Butter Tub or Ice Bucket	3.50	7.50
Cocktail Shaker	4.50	10.00
Cup	1.50	1.75
Creamer, Footed	1.75	2.50
Decanter and Stopper	8.50	15.00
Goblet, 7" to 8" (Varies)		
9 oz.	3.50	4.50
Pitcher, 8", 60 oz.	7.00	10.00
*Pitcher, 8½", 80 oz.	7.50	13.00
Plate, 6¼" Sherbet	.75	1.00
Plate, 6", Off Center Ring	1.00	1.25
**Plate, 8" Luncheon	1.00	1.25
***Salt and Pepper, Pr., 3"	6.00	12.00

	CRYSTAL	CRYSTAL DECOR. GREEN
Sandwich Server		
Center Handle	3.50	10.00
Saucer	.75	1.25
Sherbet, Low		
(for 6½" Plate)	1.00	1.50
Sherbet, 4¾" Footed	2.50	3.50
Sugar, Footed	1.75	2.50
Tumbler, 3½", 5 oz.	1.50	2.00
Tumbler, 4¼", 9 oz.	1.75	2.25
Tumbler, 5⅛", 12 oz.	2.50	3.00
Tumbler, 3½", Footed, Cocktail	1.75	2.25
*Tumbler, 5½", Footed, Water	2.25	3.50
Tumbler, 6½", Footed, Iced Tea	3.25	6.00
Whiskey, 2", 1½ oz.	2.00	2.50

*Also found in Pink. Priced as Green.

**Red — 9.50. Blue — 9.50.

***Green — 37.50.

157

ROCK CRYSTAL, "EARLY AMERICAN ROCK CRYSTAL"

(pink, green, cobalt, red, yellow, amber, blue-green, crystal, etc. See paragraph listing below.)

McKEE GLASS COMPANY 1920's and 1930's in colors

As much as I hated to break up a good thing, I needed four pages for this pattern to do it justice; so next book this is what I will do.

I'm sure you saw the slag red footed bowl and the large blue berry bowl in the silver holder when you studied the cover. If your mind has sufficiently recovered from those pieces and all the colors shown here, then you might wish to turn back to the page of rare glass to see another style pitcher in amber and the little crystal salt dip hidden near the red Moondrops butter dish.

In my last book, red was the rage; this one hopes to show you that red is only the beginning! The photograph shows the true color of every piece with the possible exception of the yellow bowl on the left. It's a vivid vaseline color much like the lamp shown last year.

I have divided colors into three columns this year for pricing purposes. A list of colors include: four shades of green, aqua-marine, vaseline yellow, amber, pink and satin frosted pink, red slag, red, amberina red, crystal, frosted crystal, crystal with goofus decoration, crystal with gold decoration, amethyst, milkglass, blue, frosted or "Jap" blue, and cobalt blue.

The frosted blue bowl has a black stand that is typical of McKee. The large blue berry on the silver stand has six small bowls on stands to match it.

Has anyone a mate for the green shaker pictured?

The red slag bowl will visit all the shows I will attend in the future save for those trips which involve the friendly skies. Glass and air terminal inspection posts tends to make me a little nervous anyway; and the size of this would almost require an extra suitcase!

A red rock crystal tid bit server was reported to me just before going to press else we'd have tried to get it photographed. It's reported to be ruby red, 10 3/4 inches tall, having a bottom plate of 11 inches in diameter and a top plate of 8 ½ inches. The center handle is chrome and the plates both have ground bottoms. It sounds exciting, n'est-ce pas?

	CRYSTAL	GREEN AMBER PINK	RED & OTHER COLORS		CRYSTAL	GREEN AMBER PINK	RED & OTHER COLORS
*Bon Bon, 7½", S. E.	5.50	9.00	15.00	Plate, 6" Bread and Butter, S.E.	1.50	2.50	5.00
Bowl, 4", 4½", 5" Fruit, S. E.	3.00	5.00	12.00	Plate, 7½", 8½" Salad, P.E. & S.E.	2.25	4.00	9.00
**Bowl, 5" Finger Bowl with 7" Plate, P.E.	6.00	9.50	15.00	Plate, 9", 10½", 11½" Cake, S.E. (small center design)	4.00	8.00	15.00
Bowl, 7" Pickle or Spoon Tray	5.00	10.00	13.00	Plate, 10½" Dinner, S.E. (large center design)	3.25	7.00	13.00
Bowl, 7", 8" Salad, S.E.	6.00	12.00	22.50	Salt and Pepper (2 styles)	20.00	35.00	
Bowl, 9", 10½" Salad, S.E.	7.00	15.00	32.50	Salt Dip	3.50		
Bowl, 11½" Two Part Relish	6.00	12.00	20.00	Sandwich Server Center Handled	6.00	15.00	30.00
Bowl, 12" Oblong Celery	7.00	12.00	20.00	Saucer	1.50	2.50	4.00
***Bowl, 12½" Footed Center Bowl	15.00	30.00	75.00	Sherbet or Egg, 3½ oz., Footed	4.50	8.00	15.00
Bowl, 13" Roll Tray	7.50	15.00	25.00	Stemware, 1 oz., Footed Cordial	5.50	11.00	22.00
Bowl, 14" Six Part Relish	9.00	17.50	35.00	Stemware, 2 oz., 3 oz., Footed Wines	6.00	12.50	25.00
Candelabra, Two Lite	9.00	15.00	30.00	Stemware, 3½ oz., Footed Cocktail	5.00	11.00	22.50
Candelabra, Three Lite	10.00	17.50	35.00	Stemware, 6 oz., Footed Champagne	5.00	11.00	20.00
Candlestick, 5½" Low, Pr.	9.00	13.00	30.00	Stemware, 8 oz., Large Footed Goblet	7.00	15.00	30.00
Candlestick, 8½" Tall, Pr.	12.00	25.00	47.50	Sundae, 6 oz. Low Footed	5.25	11.00	20.00
Candy and Cover, Round	12.50	25.00	60.00	Sugar, 10 oz. Open	5.00	10.00	20.00
Cake Stand, 11", Footed, 2¾" High	7.00	17.00	35.00	Sugar, 10 oz., Covered	10.00	20.00	30.00
Comport, 7"	5.00	9.00	20.00	Tumbler, 2½ oz., Whiskey	3.50	10.00	20.00
Creamer, 9 oz., Footed	5.50	9.50	17.50	Tumbler, 5 oz. Juice	7.00	9.00	17.50
Cruet and Stopper, 6 oz. Oil	20.00	35.00	55.00	Tumbler, 5 oz., Old Fashioned	4.50	10.00	20.00
Cup, 7 oz.	3.50	7.00	15.00	Tumbler, 9 oz., Concave or Straight	4.00	10.00	20.00
Goblet, 7½ oz., 8 oz. Low Footed	7.00	14.00	23.50	Tumbler, 12 oz., Concave or Straight	4.50	12.50	25.00
Goblet, 11 oz., Low Footed, Iced Tea	8.00	15.00	25.00	Vase, 11" Footed	12.00	35.00	70.00
Jelly, 5" Footed, S.E.	5.00	9.00	17.50				
Lamp, Electric	35.00	70.00	100.00				
Parfait, 3½ oz., Low Footed	3.00						
Pitcher, ½ Gal., 7½" High	20.00						
Pitcher Large	25.00						

*S.E. McKee designation for scalloped edge
**P.E. McKee designation for plain edge
***Red Slag — $250.00. Cobalt — $125.00.

Please refer to Foreword for pricing information

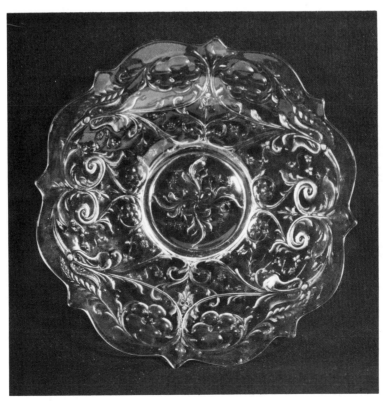

159

ROSE CAMEO

(green)

BELMONT TUMBLER COMPANY

1931

Rose Cameo is often confused with Cameo by beginning collectors. Notice this has a rose in the cameo rather than the dancing girl. This confusion occurs especially when ordering glass; so you might ask the seller whether the piece has a dancing girl or a rose within the Cameo. I once ordered an ice tub in Rose Cameo that turned out to be Cameo; I, at least, came out of that deal smelling like the rose I ordered.

A new style 5 inch bowl having straight sides was reported to me. The one pictured in the center has rounded sides; so look for the newer listed bowl in this not so plentiful pattern.

	GREEN		GREEN
Bowl, 4½″ Berry	1.25	Sherbet	1.50
Bowl, 5″ Cereal	1.50	Tumbler, 5″, Footed (2 Styles)	4.00
Plate, 7″ Salad	1.50		

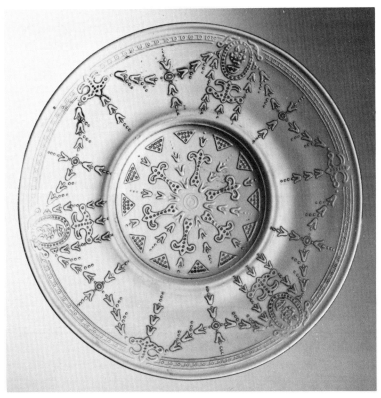

161

ROSEMARY, "DUTCH ROSE"

(pink, green, amber)

FEDERAL GLASS COMPANY
1935-37

All the pieces shown here in Rosemary represent the outcome of Federal's twice restyling the Mayfair pattern it had when Hocking got the patent on the "Mayfair" name first. As pointed out in the write up on Federal's Mayfair, the Rosemary pattern doesn't have the arches around the base of the items, nor does it have the honeycomb in the arches between the designs.

Rosemary is found in amber, pink and green; but I have never seen any in crystal, so I've taken that color out this time.

Another real oddity in Rosemary is the fact that the sugar bowls do not have handles; rather, they resemble a footed tumbler or sherbet. Even as I write this, however, an image of a one-handled sugar (lip-less creamer?) I saw in amber years ago is flashing in my mind. So, pay attention and help me prove I wasn't just dreaming.

Pink Rosemary is catching up in popularity with green. Cream soups and oval vegetable bowls are the hardest pieces to find though the 6 inch cereal bowls and the tumblers won't exactly jump into your arms.

This pattern seems to have been used extensively as most pieces you find are badly scratched.

If more of this were available, I believe it would be a widely collected pattern.

	AMBER	PINK/ GREEN		AMBER	PINK/ GREEN
Bowl, 5" Berry	1.50	3.00			
Bowl, 5" Cream Soup	4.00	9.50	Plate, Dinner	2.50	5.00
Bowl, 6" Cereal	3.50	5.00	Plate, Grill	2.00	4.25
Bowl, 10" Oval Vegetable	6.00	8.00	Platter, 12" Oval	4.50	8.00
Creamer, Footed	4.00	6.00	Saucer	1.00	1.75
Cup	2.00	4.00	Sugar, Footed	3.50	6.00
Plate, 6¾" Salad	1.50	2.50	Tumbler, 4¼", 9 oz.	6.00	9.50

ROULETTE, "MANY WINDOWS"

(crystal, pink, green)

HOCKING GLASS COMPANY

1935-39

Can't you see some prim little old lady re-naming her pattern "many windows" so she wouldn't have to tell her friends it was called Roulette!

This is the pattern for all of you who are in-clined toward liquid refreshment as there are tumblers for any size glass of lemonade or milk you prefer. There's also a nice little whiskey or shot glass for those whose im-bibing takes other forms.

Possibly the dearth of any sugar, creamer or shakers has caused people to shy away from collecting this pattern.

There is a cobalt tumbler with an embossed rather than impressed design which re-sembles the Roulette pattern. Those of you who collect this might be interested in having those even though they were not made by Hocking.

	PINK, GREEN, CRYSTAL
Bowl, 9" Fruit	6.00
Cup	2.25
Pitcher, 8", 64 oz.	16.00
Plate, 6" Sherbet	1.00
Plate, 8½" Luncheon	1.75
Plate, 12" Sandwich	3.50
Saucer	1.50

	PINK, GREEN, CRYSTAL
Sherbet	2.00
Tumbler, 3¼", 5 oz. Juice	3.00
Tumbler, 3¼", 8 oz.	
Old Fashioned	4.25
Tumbler, 4⅛", 9 oz. Water	4.50
Tumbler, 5⅛", 12 oz. Iced Tea	8.00
Tumbler, 5½", 10 oz. Footed	8.00
Whiskey, 2½", 1½ oz.	5.00

Please refer to Foreword for pricing information

"ROUND ROBIN"

(green, crystal, iridescent)

1927-32

I hated to show two "Round Robin" creamers and no sugar, but I just didn't find one in my travels. You can see a sugar pictured in the black and white photograph we took for the other books, however.

This drip tray is the only other found in our Depression Glass besides Cameo. This particular one came from Pittsburg which leads us to conjecture that "Round Robin" was manufactured by one of the numerous companies in that vicinity.

There are so few pieces of any description that it's doubtful a catalogue listing will ever turn up; but who knows? The company listing may be found tomorrow.

	GREEN	IRIDESCENT		GREEN	IRIDESCENT
Bowl, 4" Berry	1.00	1.50	Plate, 6" Luncheon	1.50	1.75
Cup, Footed	2.00	2.25	Plate, 12" Sandwich	3.00	3.75
Creamer, Footed	3.00	3.25	Saucer	1.00	1.00
Domino Tray	10.00		Sherbet	2.00	2.25
Plate, 6" Sherbet	1.00	1.00	Sugar	3.00	3.25

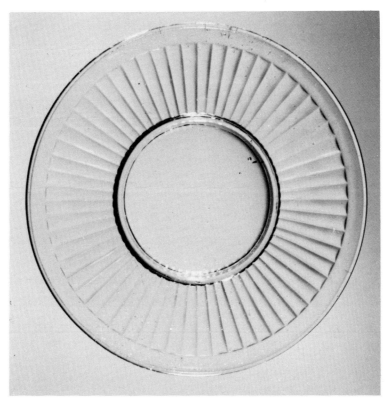

167

ROXANA

(yellow, white, crystal)

HAZEL ATLAS GLASS COMPANY
1932

You will find dealers who won't recognize Roxana as it turns up too rarely to make it worth their while to remember. No matter how rare a piece of glass is, if there is little demand for it, the prices will stay down. Roxana grows on you, however, when given the chance.

I have had the little white bowl for a very long time and have only seen one other; so they must not be too common.

You have a "ghost of a chance" to find that phantom cup; so far no one has found one real enough to drink from, however.

	YELLOW	WHITE
Bowl, 4½" x 2⅜"	3.00	9.00
Bowl, 5" Berry	2.50	
Bowl, 6" Cereal	3.50	

	YELLOW
Plate, 6" Sherbet	2.00
Saucer	1.50
Sherbet, Footed	2.00
Tumbler, 4", 9 oz.	4.50

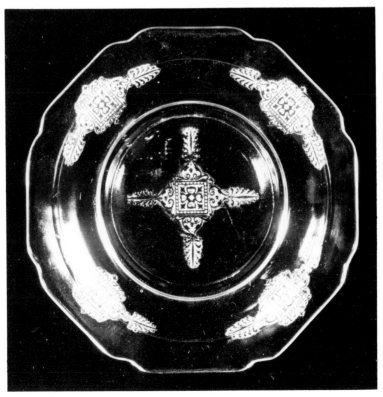

ROYAL LACE

(pink, green, crystal, blue, amethyst)

HAZEL ATLAS GLASS COMPANY
1934-41

After looking at all those old green Royal Lace pitchers in the past, I thought you might like to see the various colors of salt shakers and butter dishes for a change!

Collecting cobalt blue has again become fashionable. For a while, only green was being collected and blue sat on dealer's tables due to its higher prices. Now that green prices have caught up with the blue, dealer's can sell blue once again. Since neither color is cheap, collectors are turning to crystal and pink.

This pattern is intricately designed and the crystal shows this to advantage. Gone, however, are the days when the crystal sold for less than the pink. In fact, tumblers, shakers and butter dishes are harder to find in crystal than in pink; and how many covered sugars have you seen lately in crystal?

Tall iced teas and little juice glasses in all colors have disappeared into collector's homes, I suppose; you certainly don't see them in dealer's booths.

The hot toddy or cider set pictured in amethyst is missing the red knobbed ladle. You will find this set with the 6 roly-poly cups and the metal lid in cobalt also. A friend was gleefully bragging about having found his set at a garage sale for $20.00 when his neighbor got up and left; in a few minutes she returned with hers which still had the original sticker price of 98¢ on it. She'd received hers as a gift when she graduated from college in 1938; she'd only recently run into it while cleaning the attic. It had never been used; but until that conversation, she'd planned to throw it out. Mother would have exclaimed over how tacky it was to give a gift with the price attached; but how interesting for us, right? Has your attic been cleaned lately?

	CRYSTAL PINK	GREEN	BLUE
Bowl, 4¾" Cream Soup	4.00	6.00	10.00
Bowl, 5" Berry	4.00	8.50	9.00
Bowl, 10" Round Berry	6.00	13.50	17.50
Bowl, 10", 3 Leg, Straight Edge	9.00	20.00	22.00
Bowl, 10", 3 Leg, Rolled Edge	10.00	22.50	27.50
Bowl, 10", 3 Leg, Ruffled Edge	12.00	22.50	27.50
Bowl, 11" Oval Vegetable	6.00	10.00	15.00
*Butter Dish and Cover	65.00	185.00	185.00
Candlestick, Pr., Straight Edge	12.00	25.00	30.00
Candlestick, Pr., Rolled Edge	16.00	35.00	35.00
Candlestick, Pr., Ruffled Edge	17.00	35.00	35.00
Cookie Jar and Cover	15.00	20.00	55.00
Creamer, Footed	4.00	7.50	14.50
Cup	3.00	6.00	8.00
Pitcher, 54 oz., Straight Sides	27.50	50.00	45.00
Pitcher, 8", 68 oz.	25.00	55.00	60.00
Pitcher, 8", 86 oz.	32.50	75.00	65.00

*Butter Dish in Crystal — $40.00

	CRYSTAL PINK	GREEN	BLUE	AMETHYST
Pitcher, 8½", 96 oz.	37.50	90.00	85.00	
Plate, 6" Sherbet	1.50	2.50	3.50	
Plate, 8½" Luncheon	2.50	4.00	8.50	
Plate, 10" Dinner	3.00	7.00	10.00	
Plate, 9⅞" Grill	3.00	7.00	10.00	
Platter, 13" Oval	6.00	12.00	17.50	
Salt and Pepper, Pr.	25.00	67.50	100.00	
Saucer	1.50	2.00	3.50	
Sherbet, Footed	2.50	8.00	10.00	
Sherbet in Metal Holder			11.00	25.00
Sugar	4.00	7.50	14.50	
Sugar Lid	7.50	12.50	25.00	
Tumbler, 3½", 5 oz.	5.00	13.00	15.00	
Tumbler, 4⅛", 9 oz.	5.00	12.50	14.00	
Tumbler, 4⅞", 12 oz.	7.00	15.00	15.00	
Tumbler, 5⅜", 13 oz.	9.00	16.00	16.00	
Toddy or Cider Set: Includes Cookie Jar, Metal Lid, Metal Tray, 8 Roly-Poly Cups and Ladle			85.00	85.00

Please refer to Foreword for pricing information

Factory experimental plate.

ROYAL RUBY

(red)

ANCHOR HOCKING GLASS COMPANY
1939-1960's

A large portion of people who collect Royal Ruby glassware do so for the color alone. They don't really care what pattern the glass is, as long as it's red. You can find pieces of it in many of Hocking's glass patterns. When I first started buying glass, in 1970, you ran into Royal Ruby practically everywhere you went; I am amazed at how rapidly it's disappearing as buyer's greedily gobble it up. As I said, some buy it for no reason other than they like red glass; I've had a few people tell me they got it to set the table with on special occasions, especially Christmas.

Goblets, footed wine glasses, footed creamers and sugars and all the pitchers and round shaped items are rapidly disappearing. The later issued, squared dishes are slower at leaving the dealer's table; but they eventually sell. You also will find the squared items in a color called "Forest Green" which is becoming collectible.

When did you last see a flat soup in Royal Ruby?

In the past I admonished beginning collectors to take note of this glass as it was reasonably priced and readily available; however, I can already see the tide going out; so if there is something you particularly want in this red glassware, you'd better be getting it now.

	RED
Ash Tray, 4½" Square	2.00
Bowl, 4¼" Berry	2.00
Bowl, 7½" Soup	5.00
Bowl, 8" Oval Vegetable	6.00
Bowl, 8½" Large Berry	6.00
Creamer, Flat	3.50
Creamer, Footed	5.00
Cup (Round or Square)	2.25
Goblet, Ball Stem	6.00
Lamp	15.00
Pitcher, 42 oz., Tilted or Upright	10.00
Pitcher, 3 qt., Tilted or Upright	15.00
Plate, 6½" Sherbet	1.25
Plate, 7" Salad	2.00
Plate, 7¾" Luncheon	2.50
Plate, 9" or 9¼" Dinner	3.50
Punch Bowl and Stand	20.00

	RED
Punch Cup	2.25
Saucer (Round or Square)	1.00
Sherbet, Footed	3.00
Sugar, Flat	3.50
Sugar, Footed	5.00
Tumbler, 3½ oz. Cocktail	3.50
Tumbler, 5 oz., Juice, 2 Styles	3.00
Tumbler, 9 oz. Water	3.50
Tumbler, 10 oz. Water	4.00
Tumbler, 13 oz. Iced Tea	6.00
Tumbler, 2½ oz. Footed Wine	6.00
Vase, 4" Ball Shaped	3.00
Vase, 6½" Bulbous, Tall	7.00
Vases, Several Styles (Small)	4.00
Vases, Several Styles (Large)	6.00

173

"S" PATTERN, "STIPPLED ROSE BAND"

(pink, crystal, green, amber)

MACBETH EVANS GLASS COMPANY
1930-33

Evidently pink "S" Pattern has either disappeared entirely or it hides when I'm looking for it. A pink creamer and sugar are the only pieces I've seen in the last year.

The cherry red plate is the only piece in 'true' red glass to show up in "S" Pattern; thus, it is being collected only for its rarity and color since there seem to be no other pieces available in it.

Fired on red items are showing up more frequently; but, as is the case with most fired on colors, there are not many collectors for it.

Although most pitchers that are found in "S" Pattern have a mold etched pattern, that silk screen process used on the Dogwood pitchers was also tried on some in "S" Pattern; so far, these have only been noticed in green. Observe how heavy the pattern is on the green tumbler where the silk screen process was used.

Only the 6 inch plate in monax continues to be seen. So, the same thing that was said about the 8 inch red plate holds true for this.

Demand for the crystal with trims of silver, blue, green, amber or orchid continues to be greater than for the plain crystal; thus the prices for those pieces are also higher.

	YELLOW, AMBER, CRYSTAL	CRYSTAL WITH TRIMS
*Bowl, 5½" Cereal	1.50	2.00
Bowl, 8½" Large Berry	3.50	4.00
*Creamer, Thick or Thin	2.00	2.50
*Cup, Thick or Thin	1.50	1.75
Pitcher, 80 oz. (Like "Dogwood") (Green: 250.00)	27.50	30.00
Pitcher, 80 oz. (Like "American Sweetheart")	40.00	45.00
Plate, 6" Sherbet (Monax: 17.00)	1.00	1.25
**Plate, 8" Luncheon	1.50	1.75
Plate, 9¼" Dinner	2.00	2.50
Plate Grill	1.50	1.75
Plate, 11" Heavy Cake	20.00	20.00
Plate, 13" Heavy Cake	37.50	30.00
*Saucer	1.00	1.25
Sherbet, Low Footed	2.00	2.50
*Sugar, Thick and Thin	2.00	2.50
Tumbler, 3½", 5 oz.	2.25	3.50
Tumbler, 4", 9 oz. (Green: 30.00)	2.50	3.75
Tumbler, 4¼", 10 oz.	3.00	4.00
Tumbler, 5", 12 oz.	3.50	5.00

*Fired-on red items will run approximately three times price of amber.
**Deep Red — $60.00.

Please refer to Foreword for pricing information

SANDWICH

HOCKING GLASS COMPANY
1939-64

Green pitchers in Sandwich have always been hard to find; but the larger, half gallon pitcher has really become cloistered! There's a story as to why this scarcely twenty year old pitcher is rare. Five pieces were packed in oats, the juice glasses and tumblers being among those. Since these were the days before instant cereals, nearly everyone had a set of glasses for which they needed a pitcher. However, someone tried to promote pitcher and tumbler sets in the stores and people wouldn't buy them. They had the glasses already. So, if you want one of these pitchers, the time to get it is when you see it, I know. I passed one up thinking I'd get it before I left and the dealer sold it before I got out of sight. I haven't been able to find one since.

All other pieces in green Sandwich can be found with a little searching. I might mention that you may not find a green cookie jar top since memory serving one of the workers says it was sold as a vase. On the other hand, I've been told more than once that they do exist. I haven't seen one.

The small custard liner in green was part of that oats premium thing, so you find them in green; however, the liner in crystal is hard to find. The custard and small berry dish were included as oats premiums, also. Butter dishes were very plentiful in the past; however, the supply has noticeably dwindled.

I have also heard from people who are interested in having the crystal sandwich cookie jar which appeared in the August 4, 1975, issue of Newsweek. For the most part, these are not collectors per se; they're just finding it to be an attractive piece of glass.

The opaque white punch bowl set was a premium sold at a nominal price when you had your car's oil changed at the local garage. Most of these have a gold rim.

Hocking made:

Crystal	1930-1960's	Pink	
Amber (Desert Gold)	1960's	Ruby Red	
	1939-40	Forest Green	1950's-60's
	1939-40	White (Opaque)	1950's

	CRYSTAL	DESERT GOLD	RUBY RED	FOREST GREEN	PINK
Bowl, 4⅞" Berry	1.00	2.00	7.50	1.25	2.00
Bowl, 6" Cereal	1.50	2.50			
Bowl, 6½" Smooth or Scallopped	1.50	3.50		8.00	
Bowl, 7" Salad	2.00			12.00	
Bowl, 8" Smooth or Scalloped	2.50		20.00	14.00	5.00
Bowl, 8¼" Oval	3.00				
Butter Dish, Low	20.00				
Cookie Jar and Cover	20.00	22.50		15.00†	
Creamer	2.00			12.00	
Cup, Tea or Coffee	1.25	3.00		7.00	
Custard Cup	1.00			1.00	
Custard Cup Liner	4.00			1.00	

	CRYSTAL	DESERT GOLD	FOREST GREEN
Pitcher, 6" Juice	27.50		60.00
Pitcher, ½ gal., Ice Lip	32.50		125.00
Plate, 7" Dessert	1.25	1.75	
Plate, 9" Dinner	1.50	2.75	11.00
Plate, 9" Indent For Punch Cup	2.00		
Plate, 12" Sandwich	2.50	6.00	
Saucer	1.00	1.50	2.50
Sherbet, Footed	3.00		
Sugar and Cover	4.00		12.00†
Tumbler, 5 oz. Juice	1.25		1.50
Tumbler, 9 oz. Water	2.25		2.00
Tumbler, 9 oz. Footed	2.50		

†(No Cover)

SANDWICH

(crystal, amber, pink, red, teal blue, light green) **INDIANA GLASS COMPANY 1920's - 1970's**

After a lot of searching for glassware, I have come to the conclusion that there isn't enough of the pink, green or the original golden amber shown by the plate in the background to collect into sets. You may find a piece or two to buy, but hardly more than that. If by some twist of fate you have a complete set in one of those colors, call me collect; it would be worth it to get it photographed. Since none has been offered for sale to speak of, I intend to price only those items I've actually seen or have seen advertised.

I know at least three items in red Sandwich date from 1933, i.e. cups, creamers and sugars. I suppose we may assume a saucer was made for the cups. I know this because these items are found with inscriptions for the 1933 World's Fair.

Teal blue Sandwich dates from the 1950's and the supply is very limited; thus the higher prices on some of the more desirable items.

In 1969, the Tiara Home Products line produced the following items in red: pitchers, 9 ounce goblets, cups and saucers, wines and wine decanter with a 13 inch serving plate, creamers and sugars and salad and dinner plates.

Now, having said all that, I'm not going to stick my neck out and say these 9 ounce red goblets you find with these "histories" (". . . went through the '37 flood with my Aunt Annie holding them in her lap on the rooftop . . .") are any older than 1969. They may or may not be. I don't have the necessary data to prove it one way or another. A lot of old red glass turns a glowing yellow under black light due to uranium ore used in making the glass. The cup I have does this. If the newly issued glass doesn't do this, then you might see if Aunt Annie's glasses will stand this test.

One question raised with me more often this year than any other concerns the tid bit server which has two different sandwich patterns. The bottom is the 10½" plate and the top is Indiana's 6 inch hexagonal nappy. So don't let the ruffled edge and raised sides bother you; both pieces are Indiana's.

We may now have the answer to the scarcity of crystal butter dish tops. The last three "tops" I've found had triangular patterned holes drilled in them so that these "globes" could be attached to the metal ceiling plates of light fixtures.

If they won't "move" as butter dish tops, then drill holes in the sides and hang them as light fixtures. Enterprising, but hardly helpful to those of us who need butter tops.

		Pink	late 1920's-early 1930's		Teal Blue	1950's
Crystal	late 1920's-1960's					
Amber	late 1920's-1970's	Red	1933-1970's		Light Green	1930's

	CRYSTAL	PINK/GREEN	TEAL BLUE	RED
Ash Tray Set (Club, Spade, Heart, Diamond Shapes)	4.00	8.00		
Bowl, 4¼" Berry	1.00	2.50		
Bowl, 6"	1.50	3.50		
Bowl, 6", 6 Sides	2.50		5.00	
Bowl, 8¼"	3.00	5.50		12.00
Bowl, 9" Console	6.00	12.50		
Bowl, 10" Console	5.00	15.00		
Butter Dish and Cover, Domed	55.00	75.00	175.00	
Candlesticks, 3½", Pr.	6.00	10.00		
Candlesticks, 7", Pr.	10.00	20.00		
Creamer	2.00	5.00		22.50
Cruet, 6½ oz. and Stopper	20.00		90.00	
Cup	1.75	3.50	5.00	15.00
Creamer and Sugar on Diamond Shaped Tray	8.00		15.00	
Decanter and Stopper	27.50	50.00		
Goblet, 9 oz.	7.50	9.00		
Pitcher, 68 oz.	27.50	50.00		
Plate, 6" Sherbet	1.00	2.00	2.50	
Plate, 7" Bread and Butter	1.50	2.50		
Plate, 8" Oval, Indent for Sherbet	2.50	4.00	6.00	
Plate, 8⅜" Luncheon	1.50	3.50	5.00	
Plate, 10½" Dinner	3.00	6.00	8.00	
Plate, 13" Sandwich	5.00	8.00	12.50	
Sandwich Server, Center Handle	12.00	20.00		
Saucer	1.00	1.50		
Sugar	2.50	5.00		22.50
Tumbler, 3 oz. Footed Cocktail	8.00	9.00		
Tumbler, 8 oz. Footed Water	6.00	7.00		
Tumbler, 12 oz. Footed Iced Tea	7.00	8.00		
Wine, 3", 4 oz.	8.00	12.50		

179

SHARON, "CABBAGE ROSE"

(pink, green, amber, crystal)

FEDERAL GLASS COMPANY
1935-39

To save me a couple of hundred letters and you a big let down, let me make what I said in the last edition about crystal Sharon a great deal more explicit. There have been three pieces of crystal Sharon found: the footed tumbler, salad plate and cake plate. There are millions of crystal cake plates, very few footed tumblers and only three salad plates to my knowledge. If you have some other piece in crystal Sharon, please write.

Prices for green Sharon have cooled down somewhat except on the footed cake plate and the salad plate.

Salad plates have turned out to be scarce in all colors. They didn't come with the sets originally but had to be purchased as a separate item. Evidently not too many people did that.

Let's also discuss the soup and jam dish distinction. The soup bowl is 2 inches high and is shown behind the pink shakers; this is found in pink and amber, but not in green, as yet. The jam dish, located behind the green shakers, is 1½ inches deep and is the same as the butter dish bottom except the jam dish doesn't have the ledge for the lid

to rest on. These jam dishes can be found in all colors; yet the pink is rarely seen.

A cheese dish is represented by the amber covered dish in the center of the photograph; the butter dish is pink. The distinctions between these are as follows: the cheese dish has a ¾ inch raised rim INTO WHICH the top fits; the bottom of the cheese dish is more like a plate than a bowl, the butter dish has a bowl-like bottom and has a ledge UPON WHICH the top rests. I have never seen a green cheese dish, but a customer of mine says she sold one. So one must be out there somewhere.

I know one pitcher and tumbler collector who rues the day he passed my footed iced teas in green at $17.50 each. He was warned they were rare; but he was going to find them cheaper. If whoever bought those would like to triple their money now, I believe he'd be receptive to buying them. Notice that prices in pink Sharon have gotten way ahead of the prices for amber in many cases; now would be the time to collect a set of amber before you're caught saying how you wished you'd bought the amber Sharon when the prices were so cheap!

	AMBER	PINK	GREEN
Bowl, 5" Berry	2.00	3.00	4.00
Bowl, 5" Cream Soup	6.00	10.00	12.50
Bowl, 6" Cereal	4.00	5.00	6.00
Bowl, 7½", Flat Soup			
Two Inches Deep	4.50	7.50	
Bowl, 8½" Large Berry	2.25	5.50	9.00
Bowl, 9½" Oval Vegetable	4.50	7.50	10.00
Bowl, 10½" Fruit	8.50	10.00	15.00
Butter Dish and Cover	25.00	30.00	55.00
Cake Plate, Footed, 11½"	12.00	11.00	25.00
Candy Jar and Cover	17.00	20.00	75.00
Cheese Dish and Cover	60.00	120.00	*
Creamer, Footed	3.00	5.00	7.50
Cup	2.00	2.50	4.50
Jam Dish, 7½"	5.00	7.00	10.00

	AMBER	PINK	GREEN
Pitcher, 80 oz., With or			
Without Ice Lip	40.00	42.50	175.00
Plate, 6" Bread and Butter	1.25	1.75	2.75
Plate, 7½" Salad	3.00	5.50	5.50
Plate, 9½" Dinner	3.50	4.50	6.00
Platter, 12½" Oval	5.00	7.00	10.00
Salt and Pepper, Pr.	20.00	25.00	45.00
Saucer	1.25	1.50	2.00
Sherbet, Footed	5.00	4.75	10.00
Sugar	3.00	5.00	7.50
Sugar Lid	10.00	8.00	15.00
Tumbler, 4⅛", 9 oz.			
Thick or Thin	8.50	10.00	22.50
Tumbler, 5¼", 12 oz.			
Thick or Thin	12.00	14.00	30.00
Tumbler, 6½", Footed, 15 oz.	22.50	17.50	55.00

*Reliable source had one but I did not see it.

180

181

SIERRA, "PINWHEEL"

(pink, green)

JEANETTE GLASS COMPANY

1931-33

You have almost the complete story of Sierra in the picture before you. What the camera couldn't tell you is how difficult it is to accumulate perfect pieces. Oh, the nicks and chunks you find on those points that jut outward in this pattern.

I included the Adam-Sierra butter so you could see it with this set also. This butter top is the only piece of glass found that goes with two patterns. The Adam pattern is found on the outside while the Sierra pattern is around the inside of the top. Thus, with the proper bottom, the top serves for either pattern. How clever of the company, right? If not cleverness, possibly a faux pas.

Pitchers, tumblers, sugar bowls and platters are rapidly disappearing from the market. This is happening not just with the heretofore more desirable green, but with the pink, also.

This pattern sets a pretty table. It's sad that more accessory pieces were not made for it.

One note of warning. Be sure you get the proper cup with your purchases. Some folks will just set any paneled cup on the saucer if it "sort of" matches and the unwary are duped. Then there are some who would argue that the cup should have points on it like the plate — a condition I imagine might make for sloppy drinking.

	PINK	GREEN
Bowl, 5½" Cereal	3.00	3.00
Bowl, 8½" Large Berry	7.50	7.50
Bowl, 9½" Oval Vegetable	6.00	6.50
Butter Dish and Cover	30.00	37.50
Creamer	6.00	6.00
Cup	4.50	5.50
Pitcher, 6½", 32 oz.	22.00	35.00

	PINK	GREEN
Plate, 9" Dinner	4.00	4.00
Platter, 11" Oval	7.00	8.00
Salt and Pepper, Pr.	16.00	20.00
Saucer	2.00	2.00
Serving Tray, 2 Handles	6.00	6.00
Sugar	6.00	6.00
Sugar Cover	4.50	5.00
Tumbler, 4½", 9 oz. Footed	10.00	11.00

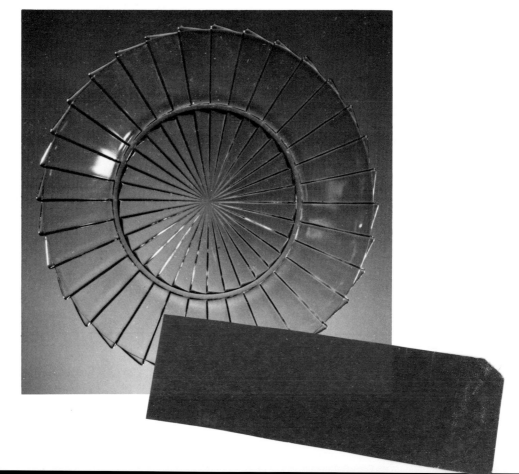

SPIRAL

(green)

HOCKING GLASS COMPANY
1928-30

I found out two things gathering the pieces for this pattern. Very few people who sell Depression Glass have any Spiral or Twisted Optic, its confusing counterpart; and of the few people who do have some, none attempt to separate the two patterns from each other. Perhaps that should have told me something; but I waded in and did fine until I got to the Spiral sandwich server. To see it, you'll have to flip over to Twisted Optic.

Before, I blithely stated that you could tell the difference in the patterns, particularly plates, by noticing that the "spirals" in Spiral go clockwise while those of Twisted Optic go counter clockwise. A few have troubled to point out to me however, that sometimes the swirled effect is underneath the piece and sometimes it's on top of the piece. So, depending on which direction you're looking at it, you can get the spirals to go either clockwise or counter clockwise. This brings us back to square one, a little wiser perhaps, but still with the identification problem. Now all I can say is to study the pieces shown, pay attention to anything, handles, knobs, overall shape, etc., that will clue you to the differences in the two patterns.

The flat creamer and sugar are the first ones designed for the set; the footed creamer shown represents a later issue.

This pattern is still economically priced and relatively easy to find at the not so posh shops. Those "junque" shops are good bets.

	GREEN
Bowl, 4¾" Berry	1.50
Bowl, 7" Mixing	2.50
Bowl, 8" Large Berry	4.00
Creamer, Flat or Footed	2.00
Cup	1.50
Ice or Butter Tub	6.00
Pitcher, 7⅝", 58 oz.	10.00
Plate, 6" Sherbet	.75

	GREEN
Plate, 8" Luncheon	1.50
Preserve and Cover	7.50
Salt and Pepper, Pr.	10.00
Sandwich Server, Center Handle	8.00
Saucer	.75
Sherbet	1.50
Sugar, Flat or Footed	2.00
Tumbler, 3", 5 oz. Juice	2.00
Tumbler, 5", 9 oz. Water	2.25

Please refer to Foreword for pricing information

185

STARLIGHT

(pink, white, crystal, cobalt blue)

HAZEL ATLAS GLASS COMPANY

1938-40

Serve that salad in a Starlight bowl with a holder ingeniously designed to accommodate the salad utensils! I found this bowl just one week in front of photographing. Nice, right?

This pattern has attracted a few converts of late. Were there more of the pink around, it would probably be a great seller; however, there just doesn't seem much to be had.

I'm omitting prices in cobalt blue for anything except bowls. If you have a piece other than a bowl, be sure to let me know; but, to date, bowls are the only pieces I've seen in that color.

The three pieces shown in white represent all I am aware of that color. If you know more than I, please help educate me.

	CRYSTAL/ WHITE	PINK	COBALT		CRYSTAL/ WHITE	PINK	COBALT
Bowl, 5½" Cereal	1.00	2.00		Plate, 9" Dinner	3.00	5.00	6.00
*Bowl, 8½", Closed Handles	2.00	6.00	5.00	Plate, 13" Sandwich	3.00	5.00	9.00
Bowl, 11½" Salad	9.00	10.00	15.00	Relish Dish	2.00	3.00	
Plate, 6" Bread and Butter	2.00	4.00		Salt and Pepper, Pr.	8.50		
Creamer, Oval	2.00	*		Saucer	.75	1.25	
Cup	1.00	1.50		Sugar, Oval	2.00		
Plate, 8½" Luncheon	1.50	2.50	5.00				

*Salad Set as Shown — $15.00

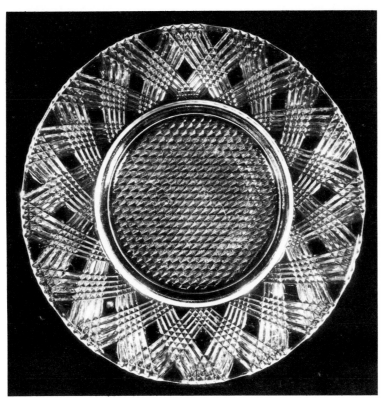

187

STRAWBERRY

(pink, green, crystal)

JENKINS GLASS COMPANY?

1929-32

Collector's have called this pattern "Strawberry" even though pieces are available with cherries in place of the strawberries. To distinguish these items, a number of dealers are now referring to them as "Cherryberry" rather than having to say "the Strawberry pattern with the Cherry design".

This is a pattern that must have been designed for the non coffee drinkers since no cups or saucers have turned up to date.

Neophytes should know that the butter bases are plain glass except for a center rayed motif in the bottom. I've heard stories of people selling Strawberry butter dishes at a reduced rate because they believed it to be on the wrong bottom. Again, the Strawberry or Cherryberry pattern will appear only on the top of the butter dish. Berry sets and the pitcher in iridescent continue to appear. I was promised an iridescent pitcher to photograph, but the collector forgot to include it with some other glass sent; so perhaps next time.

With the exception of bowls and sherbets, the Cherryberry pieces are turning out to be even harder to find than the Strawberry. This is somewhat reflected by the prices now; but it wouldn't surprise me to see them jump even more as collector's begin to notice how rarely seen they are. I've only seen two pink Cherryberry pitchers and only a few more in green. Watch especially for pitchers, butter dishes, tumblers, and cream and sugar sets.

	PINK, GREEN, CRYSTAL
Bowl, 4" Berry	2.25
Bowl, 6½" Deep Salad	5.50
*Bowl, 7½" Deep Berry	7.50
**Butter Dish and Cover	95.00
Comport, 5¾"	7.50
Creamer, Small	7.00
Creamer, Large, 4⅝"	8.00
Olive Dish, 5", One Handled	4.50

	PINK, GREEN, CRYSTAL
Pickle Dish, 8¼" Oval	5.00
***Pitcher, 7¾" (Iridescent $100.00)	87.50
Plate, 6" Sherbet	2.50
Plate, 7½" Salad	4.50
Sherbet	3.50
Sugar, Small, Open	7.00
Sugar Large	7.00
Sugar Cover	8.00
****Tumbler, 3⅝", 9 oz.	11.50

*Iridescent — 8.00

**Cherry Motif — 125.00

***Cherry Motif — 125.00

****Cherry Motif — 15.00

Please refer to Foreword for pricing information

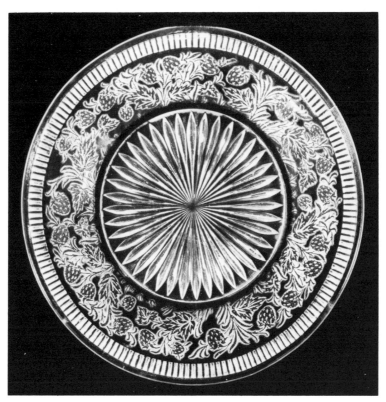

189

SUNFLOWER

(pink, green)

JEANETTE GLASS COMPANY
Late 1920's?

The cover photograph on the second edition, which is reprinted and shown in the back of this book, had the very rare Sunflower trivet pictured. Unfortunately, the first 10,000 copies printed didn't state the size of the trivet was 7 inches or that it had a raised edge. Fortunately, this grandiose omission was corrected in the next six printings; but I think about every third buyer of those first copies wrote to tell me they had the trivet. What they had, except in one or two cases, was the 3 footed, 10 inch cake plate. Again, that hard to find trivet measures only 7 inches across and has a raised edge around it; it comes in both pink and green.

Very few little ultra marine ash trays have shown up; but that evidently bothers no one at all since I took one to four different glass shows and only two people even noticed it!

The color of the creamer and sugar shown is presently unique to those pieces.

Pieces in green with the exception of the cake plate are few and far between; but as most people collect pink Sunflower, there is practically no price difference. A fair price for the ever abundant cake plate is listed here although I've seen them priced for as much as $12; but I didn't see them SELL for that. On the other hand, I was never able to get more than $2 for mine.

	PINK/GREEN		PINK/GREEN
*Ash Tray, 5", Center Design Only	2.50	Saucer	1.75
Cake Plate, 10", 3 Legs	2.00	Sugar (Opaque $75.00)	4.00
Creamer (Opaque 75.00)	4.00	Tumbler, 4¾", 8 oz. Footed	8.00
Cup	3.00	Trivet, 7", 3 Legs, Turned Up Edge	75.00
Plate, 9" Dinner	3.50		

*Found in Ultra-Marine $17.50

SWIRL, "PETAL SWIRL"

(pink, ultra-marine, delphite, amber, ice-blue)

JEANETTE GLASS COMPANY

1937-38

There are many tough-to-find pieces in this picture of Swirl. The obvious attraction, if you know the pattern, is the amber bowl in the left rear. Since this, I have also acquired that same 9½ inch bowl in an "ice blue" color. The amber one sat at the Nashville Flea Market for three months before someone pointed it out to me; naturally, I could not let an unknown color slip by, so I bought it for your edification and enjoyment, I hope.

Candy and butter dishes have always been hard to find, but the pink Swirl candy has turned out to be harder than the ultramarine. You will find the latter priced higher than pink, however, due to their being more in demand by collectors. Candy dishes, by the way, are much harder to come by than butter dishes in either color.

Two items have never shown up in pink, namely shakers and lug soups. Notice the four different tumblers down the right hand side. The pink, reported last year, is 4⅝ inches tall and holds 9 ounces. It has not been found in ultra-marine yet. The tall flat tumblers in ultra-marine are missing from many collections; so grab them when you see them. I had one collector tell me he'd looked for them so long he even doubted they existed. The very next week-end I found three and had them in my sack when I ran into him again. He had to have a peek but he didn't even inquire price as he'd turned his collection into cash for his son's college education. Yes. Some things are more important than glass.

Notice the price jumps in salad plates; and the delphite plate pictured in the right rear is 10½ inches across which is a new listing. Few delphite collectors have chosen this pattern, but delphite Swirl is more scarce than the "Cherry" delphite. Sugars and creamers are the only plentiful delphite pieces in Swirl.

	PINK	ULTRA-MARINE	DELPHITE
Ash Tray, 5⅜"	4.00		
Bowl, 5¼" Cereal	3.00	5.00	6.00
Bowl, 9" Salad	6.00	10.00	15.00
Bowl, 10" Footed, Closed Handles		15.00	
Bowl, 10½" Console, Footed	10.00	14.50	
Butter Dish	115.00		175.00
Candleholders, Double Branch, Pr.	10.00	15.00	
Candleholders, Single Branch, Pr.			65.00
Candy Dish, Open, 3 Legs	2.00	4.50	
Candy Dish with Cover	37.50	42.50	
Coaster, 1" x 3¼"	4.00	5.00	
Creamer, Footed	3.00	4.00	6.50
Cup	2.50	3.50	5.00
Plate, 6½" Sherbet	1.25	2.00	3.00

	PINK	ULTRA-MARINE	DELPHITE
Plate, 7¼"	3.00	4.75	
Plate, 8" Salad	2.00	5.00	4.00
Plate, 9¼" Dinner	3.00	3.50	5.00
Plate, 10½"			9.00
Plate, 12½" Sandwich	5.00	8.00	
Platter, 12" Oval			17.50
Salt and Pepper, Pr.		17.50	
Saucer	1.25	1.50	2.00
Sherbet, Low Footed	2.00	4.25	
Soup — Tab Handles, (Lug)	5.00	7.00	
Sugar, Footed	3.00	4.00	6.50
Tumbler, 4", 9 oz.	5.00	7.00	
Tumbler, 4⅝", 9 oz.	6.00		
Tumbler, 4¾", 12 oz.	10.00	17.50	
Tumbler, 9 oz., Footed	6.50	8.00	
Vase, 6½", Footed	4.50	10.00	
Vase, 8½", Footed		12.00	

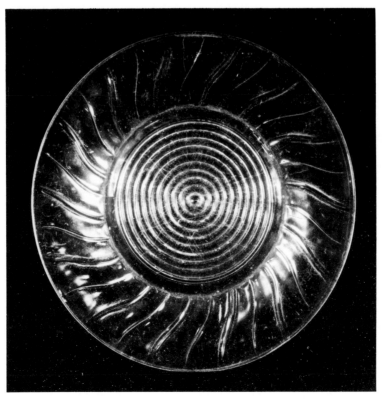

TEA ROOM

(green, pink, crystal)

INDIANA GLASS COMPANY
1926-31

The so-called Tea Room "toothpick" in the last book turned out to be a covered mustard jar with a slot in the lid and a wooden spoon. This little mustard jar can be seen on the page of rare glass at the end of the book. I apologize for the error; however, without the lid and with no listing for the piece, a "toothpick" was all I could figure it being. I've found the top in crystal, but the bottom to it has eluded me. A topless pink mustard is shown here in front of the pink shakers.

The amber pitcher, tumbler, and creamer and sugar remain the only pieces in that color to show up. The pitcher remains rare as only a very few have been reported.

Prices listed here for plates, cups and saucers are for absolutely mint condition pieces. I reiterate this because in this pattern, those particular pieces are hard to get in mint condition. One little nick, though, and the value of the piece is only about two-thirds the price listed. To emphasize the difficulty in finding mint pieces, I'll give you an example. I had the dubious pleasure of going through 32 cups, saucers and luncheon plates. Of these 96 pieces, there were only 8 in mint condition: 4 cups, 2 saucers, and 2 luncheon plates. These were all in sealed boxes and as far as I could tell, they hadn't been opened since they came from the factory. Granted, many were nicked on the points beneath the pieces; but a chip is a chip no matter where you find it.

Notice that the 10½ inch, two handled plate makes its appearance in the list for the first time.

A word of caution if you are looking for a vase in Tea Room. Find it yourself or take into consideration the extra cost of postage before you settle on a price. It's heavy, perhaps the heaviest piece in Depression Glass. So be prepared to pay a bundle if you have it shipped.

	PINK/ GREEN		PINK/ GREEN
Bowl, 7½" Banana Split	4.50	*Plate, 8¼" Luncheon	15.00
Bowl, 8½" Celery	5.50	Plate, 10½", Two Handled	15.00
Bowl, 8¾" Deep Salad	8.50	Relish, Divided	3.50
Bowl, 9½" Oval Vegetable	9.00	Salt and Pepper, Pr.	17.50
Candlestick, Low, Pr.	14.00	*Saucer	7.00
Creamer, 4" (Amber: 30.00)	6.00	Sherbet, Three Styles	3.50
Creamer and Sugar on Tray, 3½"	15.00	Sugar, 4" (Amber: 30.00)	6.00
*Cup	10.00	Sugar, Flat with Cover	10.50
Goblet, 9 oz.	10.00	Sundae, Footed	6.00
Ice Bucket	15.00	Tumbler, 8½ oz.	4.00
Lamp, 9" Electric	25.00	Tumbler, 6 oz., Footed	5.00
Mustard, Covered	25.00	Tumbler, 9 oz., Footed (Amber: 40.00)	5.50
Parfait	4.00	Tumbler, 11 oz., Footed	4.50
Pitcher, 64 oz. (Amber: 150.00)	40.00	Tumbler, 12 oz., Footed	5.00
Plate, 6½" Sherbet	4.00	Vase, 11", Ruffled Edge or Straight	12.00

*Prices for absolute mint pieces.

195

THISTLE

(pink, green, yellow)

MACBETH-EVANS
1929-30

The molds for Thistle were the same that were used for Dogwood, only the design changed, not the basic shape. Dogwood, however, has pitchers and tumblers. So far, Thistle doesn't. What a glorious find that would be for some collector!

No pitcher and tumblers leaves scant pieces to search out; and three of those meager pieces are virtually impossible to get, those being the 9½ inch fruit bowl, the 13 inch cake plate and the grill plate in particular. That cake plate is heavy and has a solid foot running completely around the underside of the plate.

The 9½ inch bowl pictured last time was in pink, but I had promised it to a collector after we photographed; unfortunately, I couldn't repeat the coup of finding another for the color picture.

The yellow cereal on the left is rather unusual because of the color. I've heard of a luncheon plate in yellow; but I haven't yet seen it.

The very real scarcity of this pattern makes many potential collectors shy away from sharing the prickly problems we encounter in this.

	PINK	GREEN		PINK	GREEN
Bowl, 5½" Cereal	5.00	6.00	Plate, 8" Luncheon	3.50	4.00
Bowl, 9½" Large Fruit	50.00	50.00	Plate, 10¼" Grill	8.00	8.00
Cup, Thin	6.00	6.00	Plate, 13" Heavy Cake	37.50	40.00
			Saucer	2.25	2.50

Please refer to Foreword for pricing information

197

TWISTED OPTIC

(pink, green, amber, crystal)

IMPERIAL GLASS COMPANY
1927-30

First, in case you missed it in Spiral, the center handled server is not Twisted Optic, but Spiral. While it's here, however, notice that the spirals in the server will match the spirals of the Twisted Optic plates and saucers. Hence the identification problem.

To further complicate the issue is the fact that Imperial is by no means the only company who made a spiraled pattern. Thus, you find any number of pieces that fit right in with this pattern, but which weren't made by Imperial. The yellow pair of candle sticks belongs in that group.

Now that we've discussed what Twisted Optic is not, there seems very little to say about what it is beyond what you see in the picture. All the other pieces there are Twisted Optic.

Frankly, its a great deal simpler for dealers to lump all of these under the heading of "one of those spiraling patterns" than it is to painstakingly designate particular patterns piece by piece; it's also simpler for the general collector as he'll have more variety of pieces to choose from; and except for the purist collector, it probably wouldn't bother either group. These aren't terribly significant patterns and the prices for the pieces in both run along the same lines. If any dyed in the wool Twisted Optic collectors simply must have only that, then study the pieces pictured and try to locate whatever identifying characteristics you can find as to size, shape, types of handles or knobs. Study the pattern listing to see what pieces the company made and then do your best at identifying pieces. That's what most of us who even try to designate patterns are doing in these cases.

	PINK, AMBER, GREEN		PINK, AMBER, GREEN
Bowl, 4¾" Cream Soup	3.50	Plate, 8" Luncheon	1.50
Bowl, 5" Cereal	1.00	Preserve (Same as Candy but with Slot in lid)	9.50
Bowl, 7" Salad or Soup	2.50	Sandwich Server, Center Handle	6.00
Candlesticks, 3", Pr.	6.00	Sandwich Server, Two Handled	3.50
Candy Jar and Cover	9.50	Saucer	.50
Creamer	2.00	Sherbet	1.25
Cup	1.50	Sugar	2.00
Pitcher, 64 oz.	8.00	Tumbler, 4½", 9 oz.	1.50
Plate, 6" Sherbet	1.00	Tumbler, 5¼", 12 oz.	2.00
Plate, 7" Salad	1.25		

199

"VICTORY"

(amber, green, pink, cobalt blue)

DIAMOND GLASS-WARE COMPANY
1929-32

Victory, by and large, has escaped collectors' attention; but it is the only pattern where collectors might possibly turn up a gravy boat and platter similar to Madrid's without selling their souls or hocking the family jewels.

The colors, especially the amber, are very vivid and you can't find the color variations within a particular color that you often find in other Depression Glass patterns. Another evidence that it is a better quality glassware than most Depression Glass is noted by the flat pieces plus the gravy boat, cup and bowls having ground bottoms rather than molded ones.

You find a variety of decoration on the pieces; some will be trimmed in gold, some have etched flowers, and some show the design found here on the console bowl and candle sticks.

There are two types of gravy boat platters; one turns up more than the other and thus is ⅜ inch narrower than the other.

Notice the matching ladle that came with the pink mayonnaise set! The green one pictured has etched flowers around its rim. Measurements for these are as follows: indented under plate, 8½ inches; mayonnaise, 3½ inches tall and 6½ inches in diameter.

You may find additional pieces than those listed; and, hopefully, **you'll** find the cobalt blue color! I was not so lucky!

	PINK, GREEN	AMBER, BLUE
Bowl, 6½", Cereal	3.00	4.00
Bowl, 8½" Flat Soup	4.50	6.00
Bowl, 12", Console	12.00	15.00
Candlesticks, 3", Pr.	12.00	15.00
Comport, 6" Tall, 6¾" Diameter	5.50	7.50
Creamer	3.00	5.00
Cup	2.50	3.00
Goblet, 5", 7 oz.	$8.00	$12.50
Gravy Boat and Platter	35.00	50.00
Mayonnaise Set: 3½" Tall, 5½" Across, 8½" Indented Plate w/Ladle	15.00	20.00
Plate, 6" Bread and Butter	1.00	1.25
Plate, 7" Salad	2.00	2.50
Plate, 8" Luncheon	1.50	2.00
Plate, 9" Dinner	2.50	3.00
Sandwich Server, Center Handle	10.00	12.50
Saucer	1.00	1.50
Sugar	3.00	5.00

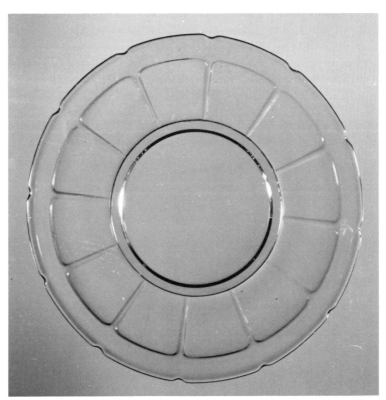

201

WATERFORD, "WAFFLE"

(crystal, pink, yellow)

HOCKING GLASS COMPANY
1938-44

Would you believe a footed crystal sugar and creamer (like those from the Miss America molds) in Waterford? Would you believe a sherbet in Waterford that is scalloped both top and bottom? Would you believe a pink Waterford goblet from the Miss America mold which even has the three rings around the top that all Miss America goblets have? Well, I hardly could either; but I've seen them all.

Shown here is a 4 inch lamp with a rayed bottom just like Waterford. I have heard reports of larger ones but the ones I've seen do not have a rayed base.

The pitcher in pink is getting elusive as are many of the pink items. I discussed how few pink butter dishes were to be seen last time; the price should prove how true that was.

Did you notice the yellow salad plate in the lower left corner?

The ash tray turned over has a "Dusty Rose" interior and the other has the "Springtime Green" interior that the Oyster and Pearls fired on candlesticks have.

"Pink shakers" turned up in Nashville, "pink" until the dealer got them home and washed them. Fortunately, they were very nominally priced; but this does point out the need to pay particular attention to the glass you're buying. I've also heard of a deal where the "green" washed off. Other cases of pricing your integrity? I feel compelled to say here that Depression Glass people are 99 44/100 percent purely good folk, indeed, the finest, friendliest people in America. However, there are those few who have the graven image of George Washington on the dollar bill ever before them, and these are the poor souls you need to be wary of.

I said before what a striking table setting Waterford makes in crystal. Well, if you could give the crystal the added touch of the red trimmed goblet shown, your guests would surely be impressed!

	CRYSTAL	PINK
Ash Tray, 4"	1.50	2.00
Bowl, 4¾" Berry	1.00	1.50
Bowl, 5½" Cereal	1.00	2.00
Bowl, 8¼" Large Berry	2.50	5.50
Butter Dish and Cover	9.00	100.00
Coaster, 4"	1.50	2.00
Creamer, Oval	1.50	3.00
Creamer, (Miss America Style)	5.50	10.00
Cup	1.25	4.50
Goblets, 5¼", 5⅝"	3.00	
Goblets, 5½" (Miss America Style)	10.00	20.00
Lamp, 4", Spherical Base	17.50	
Pitcher, 42 oz. Juice, Tilted	8.00	
Pitcher, 80 oz., Ice Lip, Tilted	10.00	40.00

	CRYSTAL	PINK
Plate, 6" Sherbet	.75	1.50
Plate, 7⅛" Salad	1.00	1.50
Plate, 9⅝" Dinner	2.00	2.75
Plate, 10¼", Handled Cake	2.50	4.00
Plate, 13¾" Sandwich	3.00	6.00
Salt and Pepper, 2 Types	4.00	
Saucer	.50	2.50
Sherbet, Footed	1.25	2.50
Sugar	1.50	3.00
Sugar Cover, Oval	1.50	4.50
Sugar (Miss America Style)	5.50	10.00
Tumbler, 4⅞", 10 oz. Footed	2.50	6.00
Vase, 6¾"	4.00	

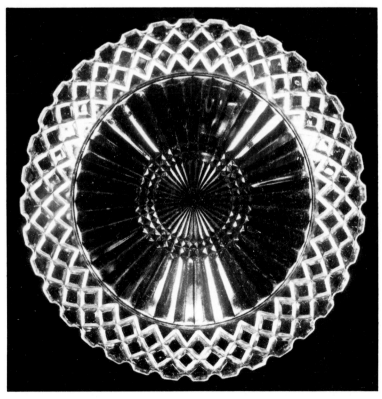

WINDSOR, "WINDSOR DIAMOND"

(pink, green, crystal, delphite, amberina red)

JEANETTE GLASS COMPANY
1936-46

This has been quite a year for Windsor as far as color is concerned! The delphite ash tray, shown also on the cover, is turned right side up here. The pitcher and tumbler reported before in amberina red are shown now. When my red "Cherry" bowl and the pitcher and tumbler were placed together, they could have been made from the same batch of glass they were so close in color. This color hasn't been "dated" yet and may never be if they were experimental pieces.

The blue plate was one of two that turned up at the Ypsilanti show a couple of years ago. The buyer even sent out for paint remover to make certain it wasn't a sprayed color!

Did you ever wonder why there were so many cups and not enough saucers to go around in Windsor. Well, the mystery may be solved if you turn to the page of rare glass in the back and see that punch bowl in Windsor! The open comport fits into the base of the 10½ inch bowl to make a beautiful punch bowl. The base of the bowl had to be designed for this comport to fit into it exactly. This punch bowl is being found with twelve cups. By the way, that comport with a beaded edge is being seen in newly made colors of yellow, red, blue and green.

The pink butter dish has gone up in price; the green has remained steady, but higher than the pink.

Notice that there are two styles of knobs on the crystal sugar and butter tops.

	CRYSTAL	PINK	GREEN
*Ash Tray, 5¾"	6.00	10.00	20.00
Bowl, 4¾" Berry	1.25	1.50	1.50
Bowl, 5" Cream Soup	2.00	3.50	5.00
Bowl, 5⅛", 5⅜" Cereals	1.50	2.00	4.00
Bowl, 7⅛", Three Legs	2.00	2.50	
Bowl, 8½", Large Berry	3.00	3.75	4.00
Bowl, 9½" Oval Vegetable	3.50	4.25	7.00
Bowl, 10½" Salad	3.75		
Bowl, 12½" Fruit Console	7.00	10.00	15.00
Bowl, 7" x 11¾", Boat Shape	5.00	10.00	15.00
Butter Dish	15.00	22.50	65.00
Cake Plate, 13½" Thick	3.50	4.50	5.00
Candlesticks, 3", Pr.	6.00	10.00	
Candy Jar and Cover	4.00	7.50	
Coaster, 3¼"	1.00	2.75	
Comport	2.00	2.50	
Creamer	2.00	2.50	5.00
Creamer (Shaped as "Holiday")	2.00		
Cup	1.25	2.00	3.00
Pitcher, 4½", 16 oz.	3.00	7.00	
Pitcher, 5", 20 oz.	4.25		
Pitcher, 6¾", 52 oz.	6.00	12.50	25.00

	CRYSTAL	PINK	GREEN
Plate, 6" Sherbet	.75	1.00	1.25
Plate, 7" Salad	1.00	1.50	1.50
**Plate, 9" Dinner	2.00	2.25	3.50
Plate, 10¼" Sandwich, Handled	2.50	4.00	5.00
Plate, 13½" Serving	3.00	3.50	4.00
Plate, 13⅝" Chop	3.00	3.50	4.00
Plate, 15½" Serving	3.50		
Platter, 11½" Oval	2.50	4.00	4.00
Relish Platter, 11½", Divided	2.50	4.00	4.00
Salt and Pepper, Pr.	5.00	8.00	25.00
Saucer	.50	1.00	1.50
Sherbet, Footed	1.00	2.00	2.50
Sugar and Cover	3.00	4.50	8.00
Sugar and Cover (Like "Holiday")	2.00		
Tray, 4" Square	1.00	2.00	2.25
Tray, 4⅛" x 9"	2.00	3.00	3.50
Tray, 8½" x 9¾"	3.00	5.00	5.50
Tumbler, 3¼", 5 oz.	2.50	3.50	5.00
Tumbler, 4", 9 oz.	3.00	4.25	7.00
Tumbler, 5", 12 oz.	3.50	6.00	12.00
Tumbler, 7¼", Footed	4.00		

*Delphite — 36.00
**Blue — 35.00

Please refer to Foreword for pricing information

204

205

SECOND EDITION COVER

AMBER	Left Center: Madrid Gravy Boat and Platter Left Rear: Parrot Footed and Flat Iced Teas
AMETHYST	Left Foreground: Iris Demi-Tasse Cup and Saucer
BLUE	Right Foreground: Iris Demi-Tasse Cup and Saucer Center: Floral Sherbet Right Rear: Princess Cookie Jar and Florentine Pitcher
CUSTARD	Left Center: Sunflower Sugar
GREEN	Left Front: Sunflower Trivet Left Center: Number 612, 9 and 12 oz. Flat Tumblers Center: Cherry Opaque Bowl Left Rear: Floral Juice Pitcher and Mayfair Cookie Jar Right Rear: Princess Footed Pitcher and Tumbler: Mayfair Liqueur
IRIDESCENT	Right Foreground: Iris Demi-Tasse Cup and Saucer
MUSTARD	Right Center: Sunflower Creamer
ORANGE	Right Center: Cherry Opaque Bowl (Reddish with yellow rim)

PINK	Center Foreground: Cameo Ice Tub
	Left Foreground: Adam-Sierra Butter Dish
	Center: Cameo Shakers
	Rear Center: Waterford Lamp by Westmoreland (pattern not included
	      in book, but shown to differentiate from Miss America
	      and English Hobnail)

RED	Left Foreground: Iris Demi-Tasse Cup and Saucer Center: Miss America Goblet
YELLOW	Center: Cherry Vegetable Bowl Right Center: Dogwood Cereal Bowl; Adam 8" Plate, Cup and Saucer Left Rear: Mayfair Juice Pitcher Right Rear: Mayfair Shakers

RARE ITEMS

AMBER	Center Front: "Apple" (like avocado) Plate
	Right Rear: Rock Crystal Pitcher
AMETHYST	Left Rear: Rock Crystal Berry Bowl
BLUE	Left Front: Floral Delphite Platter
	Right Center: Moondrops Butter Dish
	Left Rear: Beaded Block Bouquet Vase
	Left Rear: English Hobnail Lamp
CRYSTAL	Left Front: Rock Crystal Salt Dip
	Center Rear: Windsor Punch Bowl and Stand
GREEN	Right Center: Ring Shaker
PINK	Left Center: Tea Room Mustard
	Center Front: Cherry Blossom 9 Inch Platter
	Center: American Pioneer Covered Casserole
	Right Front: Adam Round Plate and Round Saucer
	Right Center: Floral 9 Inch Comport
RED	Left: Moondrops Butter Dish
ULTRAMARINE	Center: Doric and Pansy Butter Dish and Shakers
	Right Rear: English Hobnail Sherbet

COVER DESCRIPTION

AMBER   Center: Moondrops Etched Butter
Right Front: Victory Gravy Boat and Platter
Left Middle: Cherry Blossom Child's Cup and Saucer;
     Florentine No. 2 Footed Tumbler

BLUE   Left Front: Windsor Delphite Ash Tray
Left Center: Heritage Berry Bowl
Left Rear: English Hobnail Handled Bowl
Right Center: Floral Delphite Tumbler
Right Rear: Rock Crystal Berry on Silver Pedestal

GREEN   Left Center: Rock Crystal Shaker
Left Rear: American Pioneer Lamp
Right Center Front: Heritage Berry Bowl
Right Center: American Sweetheart Shaker
Right Rear: Floral Ice Tub

IRIDESCENT   Center: Louisa Carnival Rose Bowl

PINK   Left Rear: Floral Ice Tub
Right Middle: American Pioneer Covered Jug

RED   Left Middle: Windsor Tumbler
Center: Cherry Blossom Bowl
Center Rear: Rock Crystal Fruit Bowl

YELLOW   Right Rear: Pyramid Pitcher

DEPRESSION GLASS PUBLICATIONS

Below are a list of publications in the Depression Glass field which I will recommend to you as worthy of your consideration. Each will send you a sample copy if you wish to see one. Tell them Gene recommended them!

Depression Glass Daze
Nora Koch, Editor
P. O. Box 57 F
Otisville, Michigan 48463
($5.50 year — $10 for 2 years)

Rainbow Review Glass Journal
Barbara Schaeffer, Editor
P. O. Box 2315 F
Costa Mesa, California 92626
($6 year)

Obsession in Depression
Don and Norma Weaver, Editors
20415 Harvest Avenue, Dept. F
Lakewood, California 90715
($5 year — $9 for 2 years)